Occupational Case Analysis Interview and Rating Scale

Kathy L. Kaplan, MS, OTR/L
Gary Kielhofner, DrPH, OTR, FAOTA

Gary Kielhofner, Editor
MENTAL HEALTH PROFESSIONAL SERIES

SLACK Incorporated, 6900 Grove Road, Thorofare, New Jersey 08086

SLACK International Book Distributors

In Japan
  Igaku-Shoin, Ltd.
  Tokyo International P.O. Box 5063
  1-28-36 Hongo, Bunkyo-Ku
  Tokyo 113
  Japan

In Canada
  McGraw-Hill Ryerson Limited
  300 Water Street
  Whitby, Ontario
  L1N 9B6
  Canada

In all other regions throughout the world, SLACK professional reference books are available through offices and affiliates of McGraw-Hill, Inc. For the name and address of the office serving your area, please correspond to

  McGraw-Hill, Inc.
  Medical Publishing Group
  Attn: International Marketing Director
  1221 Avenue of the Americas —28th Floor
  New York, NY 10020
  (212)-512-3955 (phone)
  (212)-512-4717 (fax)

Editorial Director: Cheryl D. Willoughby
Publisher: Harry C. Benson

Printed in the United States of America

Library of Congress Catalog Card Number: 88-43518

ISBN: 1-55642-090-0

Published by: SLACK Incorporated
               6900 Grove Road
               Thorofare, NJ 08086-9447

Last digit is print number: 10   9   8   7   6   5   4   3   2

Table of Contents

Grateful acknowledgment

is expressed to the following individuals for their generous assistance in the development of this instrument:

- For co-authoring the case analysis method upon which this instrument is based and for contributing to the reorganization of the research version of the instrument, Sally Hobbs Cubie.

- For guiding the development of the OCAIRS during completion of a masters thesis at Virginia Commonwealth University, Patti Mauer.

- For assisting with the statistical analysis with the initial and revised versions of the instrument, David Bauer.

- For supporting data collection on the inpatient program at The George Washington University Medical Center, Marc Hertzman.

- For participating in the inter-rater reliability and revision phases of the instrument, Jan Magruder, Varlanda Martin, Suzanne Pickering, and Brenda Saizan.

- For conducting additional studies on the instrument for a research course at Towson State University, Anita Casales and Barbara Weinstein.

- For participating in the pilot study, Roann Barris, Rochelle Bickford, Jeanette Bird, Joanne Boyer, Ellen Kolodner, Ruth Levine, Ann Neville, Fran Oakley, and Randy Klinger-Reichler.

- For offering written feedback on the OCAIRS as used in the clinic and suggestions for improvement, Mary Lucas Bode, Rebecca Bueher, Tamera Humbert, and Muriel Leadley.

- For reviewing this manual for publication, Kathi Baron, Sandra Cohen, Patricia Michael, and Randy Klinger-Margolis.

- For participating in the audiotaping and encouraging refinement of the preliminary version of this manual, Sandra Cohen and Jan Magruder.

- For recording the audiotape, John J. Ozolins.

- For repeatedly typesetting the manuscript, Steven Glapa.

- For handwriting the case examples, my cousin, Jessica Seiden.

- For coordinating this project with flexibility and perseverance, Stephanie Scanlon and the other staff at SLACK.

- For supporting my work with love and pride, my husband, Colburn T. Cherney.

Biographies

Kathy Kaplan, *MS, OTR/L,* is a doctoral candidate at The George Washington University. Having completed her coursework in the management science department, she is currently working on her comprehensive exams and dissertation in the field of organization behavior and development. She received her BS in occupational therapy from the University of Wisconsin and her advanced masters in occupational therapy from Virginia Commonwealth University. She is the author or co-editor of three books and numerous articles.

Gary Kielhofner, *DrPh, OTR, FAOTA,* received a bachelor's degree in psychology from St. Louis University, a master's degree in occupational therapy from the University of Southern California, Los Angeles. He is currently a Professor and Head, Department of Occupational Therapy, College of Associated Health Professions, The University of Illinois at Chicago. He is the co-author or editor of five books and has published over forty articles in various journals. Dr. Kielhofner is a fellow of the American Occupational Therapy Association, a charter member of the Academy of Research of the American Occupational Therapy Foundation and has been cited for outstanding achievement by the American Public Health Association.

Chapter One
Overview of the Manual and Instrument

Purpose of the Manual

The purpose of this manual is to learn to use the Occupational Case Analysis and Rating Scale (OCAIRS). The OCAIRS is based on the case analysis method[1] for the model of human occupation.[2] The case analysis method bridges theory to practice by providing a system for collecting, recording, and analyzing clinical data. In order to use this instrument effectively, occupational therapy practitioners and students should first become familiar with the theoretical background of the model. For those already familiar with the model of human occupation and the use of this instrument, this manual provides an expanded and revised format for administering the interview and interpreting the data.

The OCAIRS is composed of a semi-structured interview, a rating scale, and a summary form. The instrument is designed for discharge planning with short-term psychiatric inpatients. The instrument provides a structure for gathering, analyzing, and reporting data on the extent and nature of an individual's occupational adaptation.

Optimal use of this instrument requires skill as an interviewer and experience in the process of psychosocial evaluation and treatment. Knowledge is also required about the content and process of the OCAIRS. This manual elaborates on the intent of the interview questions and the procedures for using the instrument. It also provides two case interviews on the enclosed audiotape that assist the learner in practicing making ratings and thinking through issues related to the use of the interview.

Target Population

The OCAIRS was developed with a sample of psychiatric patients limited to two diagnostic categories: depression and schizophrenia[3]. The nine subjects were aged 19-60 and had been hospitalized at least four days or showed sufficiently organized behavior to participate in an interview. The interview questions and rating scale descriptors were derived from clinical experience with adults in a short-term setting where discharge planning was a prime consideration.

Whether the instrument can be used in other settings or populations is a question often asked. This is a question of external validity, or the extent to which one can generalize outside of the study sample[4]. The factors that would affect generalizability have to do with the relevance of the interview questions to other settings, the appropriateness of the ratings scale descriptors for other populations, and representativeness of the content for the problems addressed.

Since there are no definitive tests for external validity, the question of generalizability can be addressed by raising other questions. For instance, is there any reason to assume that comparable measures of inter-rater reliability would be more difficult to make in a long-term psychiatric setting or day treatment setting? Probably not. At face value, the interview appears relevant to most psychiatric patients with the possible exception of a very low functioning, chronic population.

Although clinicians have expressed interest in using the instrument with adolescent and geriatric patients, the interview questions may not be as representative of adolescents' developmental issues as of adults'. Similarly, we do not know if patients in a physical rehabilitation setting would have the same type of behaviors reflected in the rating scale descriptors. Even though the overall design of the instrument is of interest to some therapists in these settings, without subjecting this instrument to further research, we cannot assume the data would be valid for such groups.

Selecting Instruments for Assessment

When evaluating an instrument for potential use, the therapist should establish selection criteria. These may include: ease of administration, relevance of instrument to treatment planning, evidence of reliability and validity, degree of standardization, resources for interpretation of results, compatibility with theoretical framework, and clinical utility. Once criteria are prioritized, review and try out instruments that potentially fit your needs.

Assessment tools collect information in a variety of ways, such as: interviews, observation, tests and inventories, performance batteries, or projective techniques. No one source of data gives a complete picture of a patient. There are always trade-offs — you may have to choose between comprehensiveness or an in-depth exploration of one or two areas. An instrument that is simple to use may also yield simplistic interpretations of behavior. An instrument that is rich in eliciting information may lack evidence of reliability and validity. An instrument that matches your own style of thinking may not make sense to the patients you evaluate or be consistent with the theoretical framework of your program.

The OCAIRS has the following characteristics that could be reviewed to fit your selection criteria:

1. It is an interview based on patient self-perception and self-report.

2. It is a screening tool that yields fairly comprehensive information about a patient's adaptive occupational functioning.

3. It provides quantitative and qualitative data (i.e., a rating scale and opportunity to record qualitative comments).

4. Data is collected and interpreted according to the model of human occupation.

5. Because the instrument operationalizes the case analysis method, it offers a structured way to learn and operationalize the basic concepts of the model of human occupation.

6. It takes between 20-35 minutes to administer and 30-50 minutes to score, record, and interpret. It is of moderate difficulty to learn and use.

7. It has preliminary evidence of reliability and validity.

8. It engages the patient in self-evaluation and individualized planning for treatment and successful community adjustment.

The interview collects information in eleven main areas:

- Personal Causation
- Values and Goals
- Interests
- Roles
- Habits
- Skills

- Output
- Physical Environment
- Social Environment
- Feedback
- Historical Data

These areas are derived from the model of human occupation and will be explained in chapter 3. Most areas have three or more questions used to elicit the desired information. The questions are written as a guide to the interviewer, but they can be reworded for the needs of specific patients or settings.

After the interview, the therapist evaluates the material in each area using the rating scale. The five-point rating scale is different from most rating scales of this type because there are specific descriptors for each number; therefore, it is important to read each descriptor carefully before selecting the most relevant rating. This will be discussed later in the chapter on Making the Ratings.

In addition to evaluating each variable of the model, the rater makes global judgments about the individual's functioning. These judgments are part of a system analysis and include ratings of:

- Dynamic Assessment
- Historical Assessment
- Contextual Assessment
- System Trajectory Assessment

The fourteen ratings give a profile of strengths and weaknesses. Until more research is conducted, there is no way to use the ratings normatively or predictively; however, the ratings and descriptions combine to give a profile of the patient that is unique to the occupational therapy perspective.

The summary form is used to record the ratings and related comments. This form gives a concise summary of the individual's occupational status. The therapist can use this data for documentation in the patient's chart.

Since one purpose of the OCAIRS is to learn the concepts from the model of human occupation, we thought it was important to keep

4

the components grouped by their subsystems. While this sequence is easier to understand conceptually, it makes the recording form a little tricky to use at first. We assume the therapist will soon adjust to the change when recording and appreciate the flow when interviewing the patient. The recording form assists in visually cuing the therapist to record starting with *interests* and to note that *historical* is addressed earlier. Still, if you want to change the form, please do so.

Why the Instrument Was Developed

With acute care psychiatric hospitalizations becoming more frequent and increasingly shorter, occupational therapists need a variety of evaluation tools that meet the predominant needs of patients in this setting. One such need is discharge planning, both to increase the relevance of the treatment process and to maximize the patient's community adjustment.

While it is critical to begin discharge planning with the initial assessment of the short-term patient, the reasons for admission frequently render the patient too confused, upset, or resistant to participate fully in an in-depth evaluation requiring paper and pencil response formats; therefore, the initial occupational therapy assessment for treatment planning may include skilled observation in both structured groups and naturally occurring settings on the unit. As the patient becomes organized and capable of reflecting on the hospital experience, more formal and in-depth evaluation procedures can be used. At this point, a clinically useful instrument would be comprehensive yet able to be administered in a short-term setting, engaging the patient in self-evaluation and goal-setting.

One means for developing such a clinically useful instrument is operationalizing the case analysis method. This method was developed as a way to help clinicians analyze case material based on the model of human occupation. Because the case analysis method is organized and conceptually sound, it offered a logical starting place for standardizing a theoretically based interview.

The occupational therapy profession values and supports the development of evaluations that have scientific properties and fill gaps in the existing methods. To meet these standards, a clinical researcher should seek to establish reliability and validity of the instrument being developed, ground the assessment in a theoretical framework, and identify current and relevant instruments in the field.

When the initial research on this instrument was conducted, 21 instruments were reviewed that were designed for adult psychi-

Table 1.1
Psychiatric Occupational Therapy Evaluations

	Projective Techniques	Observation: Checklist Rating Scale	Interview	Questionnaire	Performance
Psychoanalytic	Shoemyan Battery a, b, d, Goodman Battery a, d, BH Battery a, Magazine Picture Collage a,b,d				
Neuropsychological					SBC a,d, Person Symbol a
Developmental		Mosey Developmental Scales d,e, Allen Cognitive Evaluation b,e	*Interview Set b		
Functional Performance	Creative Clay Test a,d, *Drawing c	Mosey Checklist, *Kohlman d Comprehensive Living Skills b, *COTE a,b,d			Activity Laboratory a, *Comprehensive Assessment Process a, BAFPE a,d
Occupational Behavior			*Role History b	Interest Checklist b,d, Activity Configuration e, Occupational Questionnaire f	

Note: Instruments may be found in the following sources:

a. Hemphill, B. (1982), *The Evaluative Process in Psychiatric Occupational Therapy*, New Jersey: SLACK, Incorporated.
b. *American Journal of Occupational Therapy*
c. *Occupational Therapy in Mental Health*
d. Moyer, E. (1981), *Index of Assessments Used by Occupational Therapists in Mental Health*, American Occupational Therapy Association Special Interest Group.
e. Hopkins, H. and Smith, H. (Eds.) (1983), *Willard and Spackman's Occupational Therapy* (Fifth Edition), Philadelphia: JB Lippincott Company.
f. Riopel, N. (1981), Unpublished Masters Research Project, Virginia Commonwealth University.

* Designed for short-term setting

Adapted from Kaplan, K. (1984), "Short-term assessment: The need and a response," *Occupational Therapy in Mental Health*, 4:33.

atric inpatients within the previous 10-15 years. They were categorized into six types of instruments and five philosophical/theoretical areas[5]. At that time only six instruments were specifically designed for the short-term setting, only two were interviews, and one of the interviews and three of the questionnaires were derived from the occupational behavior tradition. (See Table 1.1). The OCAIRS represented one of the first instruments based specifically on the model of human occupation and one of the few instruments designed for short-term care with evidence of reliability and validity.

Since that time, psychosocial evaluation development has increased. For example, the Assessment of Occupational Functioning (AOF) was developed as a screening tool for use in long-term care based on the model of human occupation[6]. The Occupational Performance History Interview was also developed to be used in a wide range of settings and with various frames of reference[7]; therefore, a greater number of instruments to meet the needs of their settings, theoretical frameworks, and professional standards are becoming available to clinicians.

Benefits of the Instrument

The primary benefits of this instrument are that it is conceptually sound, clinically useful, and reasonably consistent as a measurement tool. The interview collects a range of information about a patient in an organized and comprehensive manner. The information is typically different from the other interviews administered by the psychiatric team members.

Many patients report learning from the process of the interview. The questions guide them through a unique journey of reflection on their lives.

Requirements of the Instrument

The instrument requires background knowledge and experience. Therapists not familiar with the model of human occupation will have difficulty understanding the concepts addressed in the interview.

Similarly, the process of interviewing and rating assumes the therapist is skilled clinically. He must know how to interpret nonverbal behavior and symbolic language to make sense of the patient's responses.

The instrument is largely based on the patient's self perception. Since occupational therapy involves evaluation and treatment of an individual's occupational performance, additional observation in structured group settings or with an individual task assessment is necessary to evaluate the relationship between the patient's perception and actual level of functioning.

With practice, the interview can be conducted in about 20 minutes. However, some patients need more time because they speak slower, have more to say, or need to elaborate in order to get a full picture of their situation. When learning to use the instrument, it may take the clinician longer (about 35-40 minutes) because one must decide if the response given is sufficient for rating.

Making the ratings, thinking about the patient's case, and recording the information may take a half an hour, depending again on the complexity of the information obtained and the experience of the therapist.

An Approach to Learning the Instrument

While many therapists have been satisfied with using the OCAIRS, it has not been without some initial discomfort. For example, many new learners have said they have trouble with the system analysis. Even though we developed this instrument, it still takes us a reasonable amount of time to think through each case as well. That is because this step requires critical thinking and each case represents new learning. So it makes sense that this would take some time. Of course, after much experience the therapist will begin to recognize patterns of responses and the connections come easier and faster, but in the beginning this will take some time and effort.

First you have to determine if this assessment will benefit your patient caseload enough to make it worthwhile to invest your time and effort. To what extent does it fit your plans, meet your program needs, and contribute to your professional goals and development? If you decide it is worthwhile, you might approach learning the instrument using the following steps:

1. *Set reasonable goals.*
   Skim through this manual to see how it is organized. Set aside time to read over the chapters and examine the instrument. Give yourself time to think through a plan for learning how to use the instrument.

2. *Play with the concepts first before having to do a real evaluation.*

   The audiotaped interviews make it safe for you to practice using the interview and rating scale without having to be accountable with a patient. Listen to get a feel for the interview. Follow along on the forms to try each of the steps and then compare your ratings with those in the manual. If it is more fun to do this with others in your department or elsewhere — do that.

3. *Practice giving the interview and making the ratings until you feel confident.*

   Interviewing other staff could be useful not only in developing your skill, but also in educating them about occupational therapy. Have someone interview you so you have firsthand experience in both roles.

4. *Use this manual as a resource.*

   This manual can help you identify concepts, think through issues, and make decisions. The references are provided for additional support and relevant information.

5. *Decide on how to use the instrument in your department.*

   You may want to set up criteria for how often to use the instrument and with what types of cases. Perhaps it will be a teaching tool for interns. Maybe it can be the focus of a case study in which your staff discusses the results and implications.

6. *Take time to develop increasing your understanding of the model of human occupation.*

   Read the background materials to which this manual refers. Participate in a journal club or informally discuss your reading with a peer. As your knowledge of this model develops, the OCAIRS will become an easier tool to use.

References

1. Cubie, S. and Kaplan, K. (1982), "A case analysis method for the model of human occupation," American Journal of Occupational Therapy, 36:645-656.

2. Kielhofner, G. (Ed.) (1985), *A Model of Human Occupation: Theory and Application*, Baltimore: Williams and Wilkins.

3. Kaplan, K. (1983), *Objectifying Clinical Judgment: Content Validity and Inter-rater Reliability of the Occupational Case Analysis Interview and Rating Scale*, Unpublished Masters Thesis, Virginia Commonwealth University.

4. Campbell, D. and Stanely, J. (1963), *Experimental and Quasi-experimental Designs for Research*, Boston: Houghton Mifflin.

5. Kaplan, K. (1984), "Short-term assessment: The need and a response," *Occupational Therapy in Mental Health*, 4:29-45.

6. Watts, J., Kielhofner, G., Bauer, D., Gregory, M, and Valentine, D. (1986), "The assessment of occupational functioning: A screening tool for use in long-term care," *American Journal of Occupational Therapy*, 40:231-240.

7. Kielhofner, G. and Henry, A. (1988). "Development and investigation of the occupational performance interview," *American Journal of Occupational Therapy*, 42:489-498.

Chapter Two
The Process
of Instrumentation

Research on the OCAIRS

The process of instrumentation is a long one. It is a *process* in which we adapt instruments to meet the needs of our various settings; study their utility, stability, and validity; and constantly upgrade and improve them.

By realizing the value of researched measurement tools to our professional growth and accountability, our efforts are focused on continuing the process of validation for instruments that have evidence of clinical utility. Research takes concentrated effort, energy, expense, and commitment.

Here we will review the research done on the OCAIRS to date. We further would like to invite and encourage those of you who have the interest and resources to continue the process.

The OCAIRS was developed in two phases in 1983, and the results were published a year later[1]. To determine content validity, the instrument was submitted to a panel of 15 experts who were knowledgeable about the model of human occupation and psychosocial clinical practice. They were asked to review the interview and rating scale for clinical usefulness and for correspondence with the defined theoretical concepts. Based on their feedback, which suggested the content of the instrument was valid, the instrument was revised and tested for inter-rater reliability on the research version.

Four trained occupational therapists rated nine videotaped interviews of adult psychiatric inpatients. The patients were hospitalized on the 34-bed inpatient unit of The George Washington University Medical Center where the average length of stay was two to three weeks. Inter-rater reliability, as assessed using intraclass correlation coefficient, was reasonably good for the majority of individual component ratings (Table 2.1). Based on the statistical results and descriptive data from the raters, the instrument was revised into the post-research version and later included in a preliminary manual describing the use of the instrument[2].

In the preliminary manual the total score was also used. This has been deleted in this manual because its main value was statistical. The component scores are strong enough statistically to use reliably, and the profile they create is most important clinically.

Studies by Other Investigators

Casales[3] replicated the inter-rater reliability study with four subjects with the revised post-research version. Results indicated that 57% of the components had moderate to substantial reliability coefficients (between .50-.80), 36% had low reliability coefficients (less than .50), and 7% had high reliability of greater than .80. The major factor influencing the degree of reliability was the small sample size. All the raters agreed that one subject was extremely difficult to rate. This affected the consistency of scores for that subject and the reliability of the entire instrument.

Weinstein[4] conducted a study on the post-research version of the instrument to assess a part of content validity: domain validity. A questionnaire was sent to fifteen occupational therapists familiar with psychiatric patients. The questionnaire listed eleven model components randomly ordered. Each interview question and model component was listed separately on an index card and mailed to the therapists. A percentage of correct answers matching the model components with the interview questions was used to assess domain validity.

The results indicated that 9 of the 11 components yielded 81.8%-100% correct matches between the interview questions and model components. Habits and output yielded 75% and 70% respectively. Confusion between these two definitions was thought to be due to the use of the phrase "daily routine," which is used

Table 2.1
Intraclass Correlation Coefficients

	Almost Perfect 0.81–1.00	Substantial 0.61–0.80	Moderate 0.41–0.60	Fair 0.21–0.40
Components				
Personal Causation			0.511	
Values/Goals		0.672		
Interests	0.812			
Internalized Roles	0.948			
Habit Patterns		0.766		
Skills		0.728		
Output		0.758		
Physical Environment			0.594	
Social Environment	0.828			
Feedback				0.403
Global Assessment				
Dynamic		0.691		
Historical			0.567	
Contextual		0.630		
System Trajectory				0.318

Adapted from Kaplan, K. (1984), "Short-term assessment: The need and a response,"
Occupational Therapy in Mental Health, 4:39.

in the conceptual definition of *habits*, in the interview question on *output.* (Weinstein recommended changing the interview question on output as follows, "Do you feel you have the opportunity to use your skills to the best of your ability?")

This study further supports the original study on the content validity of the OCAIRS. Although both studies should be duplicated with a larger sample, the statistical results of this study suggest that the OCAIRS has adequate domain validity for use.

Studies Comparing the OCAIRS with Other Instruments

Two studies were conducted comparing the OCAIRS with the Assessment of Occupational Functioning (AOF)[5] in an effort to further contribute to the development of the AOF and to gain knowledge about the strengths and similarities of both instruments. The OCAIRS was selected for comparison with the AOF because both are at a similar stage of development, based on self report semi-structured interviews, organized in similar formats, and based on the model of human occupation[6]. The instruments differ in that the AOF uses 25 questions to rate 20 items, with a 5–point Likert type rating scale, to measure the throughput of the human system. These correspond to the first six items on the OCAIRS. The OCAIRS attempts a more comprehensive measure, covering 14 areas total, using ordinal level ratings. The AOF attempts a more precise judgment on the components (3-4 ratings per component).

The first study[6] involved administering both instruments to 41 patients with diagnoses of schizophrenia. Numerous critical dimensions such as their psychometric properties were compared and qualitative feedback on their clinical usefulness was analyzed. The total AOF score was highly correlated and significantly positive with the total OCAIRS and comparable subsystem scores. The strong correlations support the belief that the instruments are conceptually similar.

Qualitative findings were fairly consistent and indicated that although the AOF was more quickly administered, the respondents judged the time required to be acceptable for both. Comments suggested that while both were fairly easy to use, each could be improved with clearer directions on how to use the yield for treatment planning. Both were seen as clinically useful but in need of further refinement.

The second study[7] compared the total scores of the AOF and OCAIRS with the Global Assessment Scale (GAS) to assess concurrent validity, the ability of a measure to accurately predict someone's current status. The GAS was chosen because it was easy to use, measured overall functioning, and took ten minutes to complete.

Results indicated moderate positive correlations of both instruments with the GAS, supporting the validity of the occupational therapy instruments when used to assess non-psychotic inpatients with a diagnosis of schizophrenia. Other measures of overall functioning need to be used to further research the concurrent validity of these instruments[7].

The research to date offers preliminary evidence in support of the reliability and validity of the OCAIRS. Users should be aware of some potential weaknesses, especially the lower reliability scores obtained for some items. At this point a major implication of all the research to date is the need for more development and investigation of the OCAIRS. We hope that some of you who initially use it clinically will go on to participate in its further development and investigation.

Suggestions for Further Research

Several studies of each of the various types of reliability and validity are necessary for instrument development[8]. The following are some research ideas for future instrumentation of the OCAIRS.

1. Improve the current interview and rating scale to decrease repetition of certain information.

2. Assess the predictive validity of the OCAIRS for measuring aspects of successful and unsuccessful community adjustment.

3. Compare the relative contributions of the individual component ratings and global assessment ratings to each other and to measures of adaptation such as the Katz Adjustment Scale[9]. For example, how does the rating of system trajectory correlate with other measures of adaptation?

4. Collect data on a large sample to determine whether different profiles would emerge to further refine our ability to diagnose occupational dysfunction, predict outcomes, and offer relevant treatment.

5. Examine use of the instrument with other populations, such as adolescents, elderly patients, and substance abusers. Refine the interview and rating scale as needed as an outgrowth of the findings.

6. Study the ability of the OCAIRS to distinguish healthy from emotionally disturbed populations.

References

1. Kaplan, K. (1984), "Short-term assessment: The need and a response," *Occupational Therapy in Mental Health*, 4:29-45.

2. Kaplan, K. and Kielhofner, G. (1985), *Preliminary Manual for the Case Analysis Method*, (Available from Kathy L. Kaplan, 1415 N. Hartford Street, Arlington, VA 22201.)

3. Casales, A. (1984), Unpublished Research Project, Towson State University.

4. Weinstein, B. (1984), Unpublished Research Project, Towson State University.

5. Watts, J., Kielhofner, G., Bauer, D., Gregory, M., and Valentine, D. (1986), "The assessment of occupational functioning: A screening tool for use in long-term care," *American Journal of Occupational Therapy*, 40:231-240.

6. Watts, J. H., Brollier, C., Bauer, D., and Schmidt, W. (1988), "A comparison of two evaluation instruments used with psychiatric patients in occupational therapy," *Occupational Therapy in Mental Health*, 8, (4).

7. Brollier, C., Watts, J.H., Bauer, D., and Schmidt, W. (1988), "A concurrent validity study of two occupational therapy evaluation instruments," *Occupation Therapy in Mental Health*, 8, (4).

8. Benson, J. and Clark, F. (1982), "A guide for instrument development and validation," *American Journal of Occupational Therapy*, 36:789-800.

9. Katz, M. and Lyerly, S. (1963), "Methods for measuring adjustment and social behavior in the community: I. Rationale, description, discrimination validity, and scale development," *Psychological Reports Monograph*, 14:503-535.

Chapter Three
Background
Theoretical Material

The Model of
Human Occupation

The model of human occupation is an outgrowth of the occupational behavior tradition that seeks to identify universal occupational therapy themes. Although the language of the model may be unfamiliar at first, the concepts speak to the heart of everyday occupational therapy practice. One value of the model is that it provides a common language and emphasis for occupational therapy based on the early precepts of the field. Further, the model seeks to provide a coherent conceptualization of the structure and processes that influence adaptation in occupational performance.

The concepts of the model covered in this discussion are diagrammed in Figure 3.1. The model begins with the concept of human beings as *open systems*. The concept of an open system refers to the recognition that living systems are qualitatively different from non-living or closed systems. An open system is characterized by an ongoing interaction with the external environment and the ability to maintain and change itself because of this interaction.

The Open System Cycle

The cycle of interaction with the environment includes four phases: intake, throughput, output, and feedback. *Intake* refers to the importation of energy or information into the system such as when one eats or reads. *Throughput* refers to the transformation of the energy or information for assimilation by the system and to the self-transformation of the system to accommodate the incoming energy or information. *Output* refers to the external action or behavior of the system and it results in *feedback* to the system about the process and consequences of the action. This ongoing cycle is responsible for the process of self-maintenance and self-change.

Notably, the open system cycle describes the occupational therapy process. That is, in occupational therapy, persons are enabled to maintain and change their functional capacity because of their participation in directed occupations. In open system terms we conceptualize the occupational therapy process as involving the intake of information necessary for task performance, the translation and use of that information for performance, the actual act of performance, which results in feedback to the system. Both the intake and the feedback bring new information into the system, which results in changes in the system.

While open system concepts are essential to explain some of the fundamental dynamics of human action and self-transformation, more specific concepts are needed to explain basic questions that arise about the participation of individuals in occupations. These questions are:

- Why and how do persons choose to participate in occupations?
- What accounts for the organization of behavior into adaptive patterns of performance?
- What underlies the basic ability to perform?

The Subsystems

To respond to these questions, the human being is further conceptualized as an open system consisting of three subsystems (See Figure 3.1). Subsystems are coherent functional entities that comprise a total system. Each subsystem has its own structure and function and all subsystems interact with each other. Their structure is defined as hierarchical. That means that the higher subsystems govern lower subsystems and that lower subsystems either facilitate or constrain higher subsystems. In this model the highest subsystem is referred to as *volition*; this subsystem is responsible for choosing participation in occupations. The middle subsystem is *habituation* and it is responsible for organizing behavior into patterns. The lowest subsystem is *performance*; it is responsible for producing the action of the system.

Volition

The volition subsystem is conceptualized as being composed of an underlying energy source and a set of internal images. The energy source is called an urge to explore and master. It refers to humans' universal need to explore their environments and achieve mastery over tasks and over the course of their lives. This urge thus provides the energy for participation in occupations. However, it is not enough to say that persons have energy or a need for participation in occupations; one must also account for the choices they make to participate in one occupation over another and so on. These specific choices are influenced by internal images that an individual holds about his or her self as a participant in the external world; these images are: personal causation, values, and interests.

Personal causation refers to an individual's beliefs about his or her effectiveness. They include the degree to which an individual feels in control, the identification of personal skills and the sense that those skills are efficacious for one's life situation. And, finally, they include the expectation for success or failure in the future. The particular set of images an individual has concerning

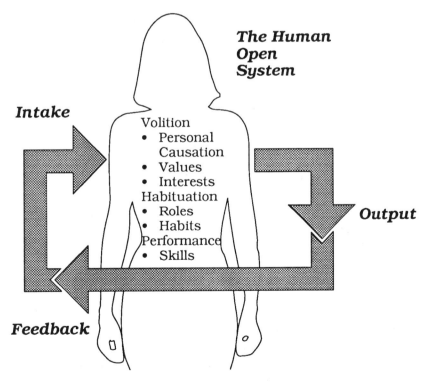

Figure 3.1
The Human Open System

From Kielhofner, G. (Ed.), (1985), *A Model of Human Occupation: Theory and Application*, Baltimore: Williams and Wilkins, p. 35.

his or her effectiveness will influence what occupations are sought out or avoided. If an individual feels externally controlled or unskilled, he or she may tend to avoid participation in occupations in order to avoid failure, but will also grow increasingly helpless and fearful. On the other hand, an individual who has a belief in internal control or skill will tend to seek out opportunities, to take calculated risks in order to achieve, and as a result will learn and grow.

Values are an individual's internal images concerning what is good and right. They provide a sense of obligation to participate in certain occupations and to perform in a specific manner. Values include one's degree of orientation to past, present, and future, and convictions about how time should be used. They include one's occupational goals and standards of performance, and the meaning attributed to certain occupations. The meanings, standards, goals, and time orientation that constitute values obligate persons to make certain choices. The person whose values generally reflect what is valued by the culture will tend to perform adaptively, while the individual alienated from the mainstream values is more likely to engage in deviant behavior. The individual with clear valued goals will be able to apply effort toward attaining them. The individual who has no goals, or who has had to give them up because of some interfering disability, is much less likely to see the relevance of performing in the present.

Interests refer to an individual's preferences for occupations based on the experience of pleasure and satisfaction in participating in those activities. To experience preferences is an essential dimension of interests. The particular pattern of interests an individual expresses will influence the pattern of choices that will be made. Finally, interests are only functional when they are potent — that is, when the individual is able to and participates in occupations of interest. Individuals who cannot discriminate interests have difficulty making choices. Persons who have narrow interests related only to work may, as a result, manifest an unhealthy lack of leisure, and many disabled persons' interests lose their potency as the disability interferes with the possibility of participating in formerly pleasurable and satisfying occupations.

Habituation

The habituation subsystem is responsible for organizing behavior of the individual into routines or patterns. This subsystem is composed of a set of images that trigger and guide automatic behavior in daily life. Two sets of images comprise this subsystem: roles and habits. *Roles* are images that persons hold about the positions they occupy in various social groups and of the obligations that go along with those positions. Perceived incumbency is the image persons have of what roles they are in.

Internalized expectations are the obligations they accept by virtue of being in particular roles. And, finally, role balance is the degree to which the persons are able to successfully integrate life roles into a pattern of living. Individuals may exhibit difficulties when they do not have roles to provide them a sense of identity and to guide their behavior, when they do not internalize appropriate role expectations, and when they experience role conflict or an overload of life roles.

Habits are images which trigger routine performances in lesser spheres of everyday life such as the habits which guide activities of daily living. The degree of organization or disorganization in an individual's habit structure will be reflected in the efficiency and consistency of daily performance.

Habits may be either flexible or rigid. The social appropriateness of habits is critical since patterns of behavior must conform, to a degree, to accepted patterns in the social group if the individual is to be judged competent.

In summary, the habituation subsystem is a set of images that trigger and guide routine performance. These images include habits and roles that interrelate in triggering automatic or semi-automatic, routine behaviors. The particular patterns of behavior that the habituation subsystem organizes, build upon and make use of the underlying skills of the final and lowest subsystem, which is discussed next.

Performance

The performance subsystem is the subsystem responsible for the production of occupational behaviors. This subsystem is composed of skills and the constituents of skills. There are three types of skills: *Perceptual motor* skills are abilities to select and interpret sensory information and effect coordinated purposeful movement. *Process* skills are abilities to deal with events in the environment through such behaviors as planning and problem-solving. *Communication/interaction* skills are abilities for dealing with people and for receiving and sharing information.

Constituents of skills are underlying structures that are used for skilled performance; there are *symbolic, neurologic,* and *musculoskeletal* constituents. Symbolic constituents refer to individuals' internalized rules for performance; they are images that guide skilled performance. The neurological and musculoskeletal constituents refer to the nervous system and the musculoskeletal system, which take in sensory information and effect motor action.

The Environment

While the three subsystems shape the output of the system, individual behavior is also highly influenced by the external environment where performance takes place. The environment is conceptualized as including four layers; they are objects, tasks, social groups, and culture. Each of these layers influences performance. *Objects* are used by persons when they perform within tasks. *Tasks* refer to both serious and playful situations for performance in the environment. Playing a game of soccer, programming a computer, stacking blocks, and driving a car are all examples of different types of tasks in the environment, each of which requires one to perform in certain ways.

Social groups refer to natural collections of individuals — for example, families, work teams, social organizations or clubs. The particular traits of the social group will greatly affect performance. Lastly, the *culture*, the values and technology that are part of the culture, are also recognized as influencing individual performance.

Summary

We have briefly overviewed some of the theoretical tenets of the model of human occupation. According to this model, the human being is conceptualized as an open system in constant interaction with the environment. The cycle of intake, throughput, output, and feedback that comprises this interaction results in maintenance of and change in the system; thus the action of the system allows the system to maintain and change itself. The human being is also conceptualized as a system composed of three subsystems. The volition subsystem is responsible for choosing, the habituation subsystem for patterning, and the performance subsystem for producing occupational behavior. Lastly, the human is conceptualized as a system performing in an environment composed of objects, tasks, social groups, and culture.

This model is based on a set of concepts developed in the occupational behavior tradition that attempt to re-energize the early precepts of occupational therapy. That means the model seeks to provide a means of conceptualizing the occupational nature of human beings, a means of understanding occupational dysfunction, and a means of justifying the use of occupations as therapy.

Resources for the Model of Human Occupation

Kielhofner, G. (Ed.) (1985), *A Model of Human Occupation: Theory and Application*, Baltimore: Williams and Wilkins.
- The "bible" of the model. Contains detailed chapters and figures on each of the theoretical tenets of the model. Discusses the model in the context of normal

growth and development as well as dysfunctions. See in particular chapter 15 for an explanation of how the model can be used as a framework for understanding patients with psychosocial dysfunction. The book contains chapters on treatment planning, occupational (activity) analysis, and program development as well as a workbook section so readers can apply the concepts to themselves and their patients. The appendix contains an extensive and well-categorized list of assessment instruments.

Kielhofner, G. (1978). "General systems theory: Implications for theory and action in occupational therapy," *American Journal of Occupational Therapy*, 32:637-645.

- Helpful for understanding system analysis and global assessment.

Matsutsuyu, J. (1971), "Occupational behavior — a perspective on work and play," *American Journal of Occupational Therapy*, 25:291-294.

- Elaborating on the occupational behavior tradition, this article is a classic and applicable to conceptualizing clinical programs based on this thinking.

Meyer, A. (1977), "The philosophy of occupational therapy," *American Journal of Occupational Therapy*, 31:639-642.

- An example of one of the early writings about occupational therapy precepts. The occupational behavior tradition is based on ideas such as these.

Oakley, F., Kielhofner, G., and Barris, R. (1985), "An occupational therapy approach to assessing psychiatric patients' adaptive functioning," *American Journal of Occupational Therapy*, 39:147-154.

- This article describes a research project designed to begin the process of establishing efficacy of the model of human occupation as an alternative to the medical model in psychiatry. A battery of instruments was used to assess adaptive functioning of psychiatric patients.

Rogers, J. (1982), "Order and Disorder in medicine and occupational therapy," *American Journal of Occupational Therapy*, 36:29-35.

- This article gives a framework for thinking about the difference between a medical diagnosis and an occupational dysfunction. Useful in clarifying and strengthening the role of occupational therapy in a variety of settings and in beginning to think about building our own taxonomy of diagnoses based on patterns of functioning.

Reilly, M. (1966), "A psychiatric occupational therapy program as a teaching model," *American Journal of Occupational Therapy*, 20:61-67.

- Reilly, as the founder of the occupational behavior tradition, gives an example of how theory was operationalized in a psychiatric training program.

The Case Analysis Method

You can see how after being introduced to the concepts of the model of human occupation, one might have a need to integrate the concepts so that they become usable in clinical practice. That is how Cubie and Kaplan developed the case analysis method[1]. We attempted to make this theoretical material usable by practicing analyzing clinical case material according to this theory. What evolved was a sequence for asking questions about the case material we had previously collected in the clinic situation prior to learning about the model of human occupation. We will review some of this method here as a precursor to learning more about the OCAIRS. In this way you can duplicate our process of theoretical development and more fully appreciate how to use the OCAIRS.

According to the model of human occupation, occupational behavior can be understood by examining the above variables and the way they contribute to an ongoing process of change, both for the person and for the environment. In an adaptive cycle, experiences support the individual's desire to explore, to master, and to fulfill the environmental demands; however, maladaptive cycles may develop in which the individual repeatedly experiences disorganization, poor performance, and the anticipation of future failure. The primary task of the occupational therapist is to enable patients to organize their occupational behavior so that adaptive cycles are learned or restored.

Data review, data analysis, and treatment planning can be organized by reference to a series of ten primary questions. Each question reflects a variable of the model of human occupation. Taken together, they encourage analysis of the entire human system for a given patient (See Figure 3.2).

Primary Analytic Questions

In the case analysis method, we developed a series of primary questions. These should not be confused with the interview questions. The primary questions of the case analysis method refer to conceptual questions that the therapist asks himself about the patient in the process of formulating an evaluation of

Figure 3.2
Data Analysis Sequence and Related Treatment Implications

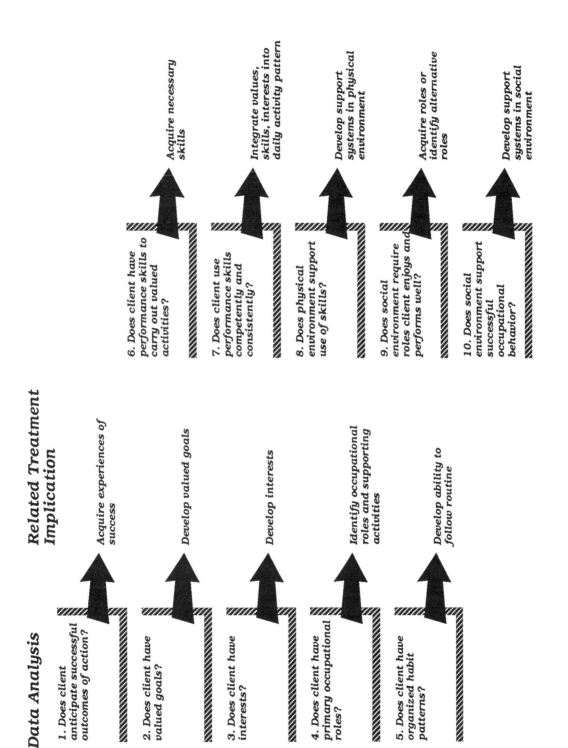

Data Analysis

Related Treatment Implication

1. Does client anticipate successful outcomes of action? → Acquire experiences of success

2. Does client have valued goals? → Develop valued goals

3. Does client have interests? → Develop interests

4. Does client have primary occupational roles? → Identify occupational roles and supporting activities

5. Does client have organized habit patterns? → Develop ability to follow routine

6. Does client have performance skills to carry out valued activities? → Acquire necessary skills

7. Does client use performance skills competently and consistently? → Integrate values, skills, interests into daily activity pattern

8. Does physical environment support use of skills? → Develop support systems in physical environment

9. Does social environment require roles client enjoys and performs well? → Acquire roles or identify alternative roles

10. Does social environment support successful occupational behavior? → Develop support systems in social environment

Adapted from Cubie, S. and Kaplan, K. (1982), "A Case Analysis Method for the Model of Human Occupation," *AJOT*, 36(10):648.

the patient. These primary questions guide clinical reasoning. The interview questions operationalize these more abstract primary questions from the case analysis method. Another way of thinking about it is that the primary questions are what the therapist asks himself, and the interview questions are those he asks the patient.

1. *Does the client anticipate successful outcomes of action?*
   What is the status of the client's sense of personal causation? Does he expect success in performance of daily life tasks? Historically, under what circumstances has the client felt effective or ineffective in occupational behavior?

2. *Does the client have valued goals?*
   Does the client have commitments and priorities for specific courses of action? Can he sustain action that might not be satisfying at present for the sake of future accomplishments? Has past behavior been goal-directed?

3. *Does the client have interests?*
   Does the client have a variety of satisfying self-initiated activities? Could past interests be renewed?

4. *Does the client have primary occupational roles?*
   Can the client describe which activities define his roles as family member, worker, volunteer, student? Have necessary role transitions been made throughout the life cycle?

5. *Does the client have organized habit patterns?*
   Does the client's daily schedule facilitate accomplishing life tasks or disorganized behavior that fails to meet basic work, play, and self-care needs? Has the client historically been able to develop necessary habits? If not, why not?

6. *Does the client have the performance skills to carry out valued activities?*
   Does the client have the motor, perceptual, and problem-solving abilities necessary to interact successfully with the environment? Have there been developmental, traumatic, or environmental stresses that have seriously limited skill acquisition?

7. *Does the client use performance skills competently and consistently?*
   Does the client use his repertoire of skills, or are some skills used poorly or not at all? Is the client a chronic underachiever or overachiever? Does the client's output satisfy his own purposes and goals?

8. *Does the physical environment support competent and consistent use of skills?*

   Do the physical attributes of the client's environment limit or encourage successful occupational behavior? Is there a history of significant poverty or wealth?

9. *Does the social environment require occupational roles that the client enjoys and performs well?*

   Do the client's family, friends, and co-workers expect the same role behavior the client expects, or are there discrepancies? Have role requirements been consistent over time or have varying expectancies caused confusion and conflict?

10. *Does the social environment support successful occupational behavior?*

   Do family and friends support the client's attempts at change? In the past, have significant individuals typically offered praise and encouragement, or criticism and conditional acceptance?

System Analysis/Global Assessments

After completing the ten primary questions, the therapist summarizes the case analysis in terms of overall system functioning.

Dynamic:	How the system is currently functioning
Historical:	How the system has functioned in the past
Contextual:	How the system is influenced by the environment

Overall System Trajectory: The direction of change in which the client is headed.

If the client is functioning adaptively, either no treatment is needed or the therapist will reinforce elements maintaining function. If the client is in a maladaptive cycle or at risk for dysfunction, then the therapist will explore and work to resolve the elements contributing to the cycle and blocking competent occupational behavior.

The case analysis method includes a form for recording case information. Each variable from the model of human occupation is addressed using the primary questions to review and analyze the data pertaining to the client. The therapist determines if the influence of the variable on the client's adaptive functioning is positive or negative and marks a check in the appropriate column. Comments explaining the judgment are written in the space provided and a check is marked in the column indicating when additional information is needed. The OCAIRS changes the positive/negative format to a five-point ordinal rating scale, offering a finer description of the client's functioning.

Reference

1 Cubie, S. and Kaplan, K. (1982), "A case analysis method for the model of human occupation," *American Journal of Occupational Therapy*, 36:645-656.

Acknowledgment is made of the source of the material from "A case analysis method for the model of human occupation" by S. Cubie and K. Kaplan. Copyright 1982 by the American Occupational Therapy Association, Inc. Reprinted with permission.

Chapter Four
Using the Interview

The Interview as a Data Gathering Method

The interview is considered a semi-structured interview. This means there is a predetermined sequence of questions and that the interviewer can reword and elaborate on the questions during the interview. This is in contrast to a standardized interview in which the questions must be asked exactly as stated without responding in any way to questions or reactions from the interviewee[1]. By the same token, the interview is not unstructured. You are not free to engage in a naturally developing conversation with the patient or to follow interesting bits of information that might lead you astray from the topic at hand.

The interview is semi-structured so the therapist can adapt it to the various patients. The questions are designed to elicit particular information tied to the model of human occupation and the case analysis method. If you modify the questions you should keep their intent in mind.

Because interviews are time consuming, they are expensive. It is important to spend the time well. Some of the guidelines below can help in this regard.

Survey interviews are commonly used and well accepted in the clinical setting and research situation. However, they are not without problems[2]. The interview situation sets up an unequal role relationship between the interviewer and interviewee. Sometimes this forces the interviewer, in the search for objectivity, to become detached. The hierarchical nature of the roles may affect the interviewee. Depending on how that individual characteristically responds to authority figures, he might be overly solicitous, guarded, or defensive.

It is up to the interviewer, therefore, to keep the context of the interview situation in mind and strive to decrease the inherent dangers. Yet, the interviewer may take on too much responsibility for the interview. He may be too responsive and unintentionally cue the patient to give certain information. Or in an effort to balance the interview, he can reveal too many of his own ideas and prevent himself from understanding the patient.

The Interviewer

To interview well takes practice. The interviewer must integrate considerable knowledge, skills, and experience during the interview. In terms of knowledge, the interviewer needs to be clear about the:

- Purpose of the interview
- Content and flow of the interview questions
- Information needed to make the ratings
- Theoretical material upon which inferences are based
- Nature of the treatment program of which the interview is a part

The interviewer needs skills for:

- Communicating effectively
- Reading nonverbal behavior and interpreting symbolic meanings
- Beginning and ending the interview gracefully
- Drawing out some responses and containing others
- Staying within the time limit established

Finally, the interviewer needs experience to:

- Know how patients with various psychiatric diagnoses reveal their symptoms

- Look for patterns in the history and presentation
- Understand the differences patients may exhibit between self-reported information and observed behavior
- Extrapolate how the actual environment might impact the patient compared with the treatment environment.

Ways to Improve the Interview

To decrease the dangers inherent in the interview situation and enhance the likelihood of gathering accurate information, several factors are necessary. First and foremost, the interviewer needs to establish trust and rapport with the interviewee. Trust is established by showing up on time for the scheduled appointment, not taking phone calls and decreasing the likelihood of interruptions, and discussing the extent of confidentiality involved. If the findings will be discussed with the team or family members, you should inform the interviewee.

Rapport is a subtle process of using the self as an instrument as well as accurately gauging the needs of the patient. The interviewer should attempt to make the interviewee comfortable through the environment, his demeanor, and responsiveness. Much information is gained about a person within the first few seconds of meeting them. Use this data to monitor how much warmth to show and how much information to share at once. People who are confused and overwhelmed need shorter sentences with limited information.

Second, because this interview relies on verbal self-expression, it is important that the interviewer ask questions clearly and clarify interviewee responses that are not clear. It is wise to think through ways to rephrase some of the interview questions so that if a patient does not understand the question, the therapist is prepared to offer a simpler restatement. Likewise, think about different ways to introduce the interview. Two ways that were used in the cases on the audiotape are presented below.

A third factor is to keep track of the time. The interview is designed for the short-term setting where patients only stay two to three weeks and are involved in multiple interactions with other staff and aspects of the treatment program. Therefore, time is precious. With practice the interview takes about twenty minutes. When learning, therapists and students have taken double that time, but with practice the interviewer can learn when to ask for elaboration and when to curtail responses. Remember, this is a screening instrument. It may be supplemented with other evaluations, observations, and forms of information at another time.

The Use of Transition Statements

Transition statements enable the interviewer to assist the flow of the interview and to guide the interviewee in how much to respond. These are statements that let the interviewee know what comes next and closes a section just completed. For instance, after collecting the demographic information, you may say something like "Let's switch gears" before asking about interests. Similarly, after asking questions about the physical environment, you may want to acknowledge that you have been focusing on external factors and that now you want to focus on people in their social world. Then ask about who the important people are in their lives.

The point is that most of the sections have several contributing questions. The interviewee may not be clear when he is elaborating on the same question or being asked something else. The interviewer has the sheet in front of him so does not experience this. Consider writing transition statements on the interview form as a reminder.

Additional Guidelines

Each individual will pose different challenges to the interviewer. The interviewer must be prepared to vary his style, pace, and phrasing as needed. Think about probes to get information from someone who is slow to respond, has limited comprehension, or difficulty hearing. Think about respectful ways to set limits, interrupt, and redirect the person who is tangential, angry, or has pressured speech.

While these are useful guidelines in conducting the interview, you will be the best judge of how to respond. Being emotionally present and attentive is most important. Each person will reveal himself in unique ways. Work to suspend judgment until the data is collected and you are at the recording and analyzing stage.

Conducting the Interview

Setting up the interview is a good time to explain to the patient the reason for the interview and what it will entail. Decide prior to seeing the patient whether you want to use background information such as a chart review or discussion with staff team members. Although knowing less about a patient may ensure a more objective viewpoint, it may be impossible and unwise in a short-term setting. The issue is to be aware of what your reactions are to the information in an effort to avoid bias.

When you start the interview, explain that you will be jotting down responses to the interview so that you can reflect on the information later. Most patients do not have a problem with that, but if they do, work out some alternative. Perhaps you will agree to give them a copy or to throw it out once the data is put into the chart. The solution depends on what meaning the writing has to the patient. Writing is somewhat distracting for the interviewer as well; however, there is generally too much information collected to rely on memory, especially when learning the interview. If you can get permission to audiotape or videotape the interview, those are reasonable options. However, the time saved during the interview is multiplied when listening to the interview a second time and recording the responses. The object is to minimize the disadvantages and accept the remaining glitches.

Introducing the Interview

Two examples of brief introductions to the interview are:

> *"Hi Adrianne. I'm Kathy Kaplan. I'd like to ask you some questions to get to know you and help you while you are in the hospital. We will focus on information to help you plan for discharge and community living. This is an opportunity for you to let me know what you need and to participate in the treatment process. I'm going to start with some basic questions about where you live."*

— or —

> *"Jasmine, this is an interview. You may have been interviewed by other staff. This is an opportunity for me to get a picture of who you are and what your life is like from your point of view. It is also a chance for you to think about your goals while you are in the hospital as well as for when you leave. I want to start by asking you a few basic questions about where you live and how you spend your time, and we will move on from there."*

Demographic Information

The interview begins with a discussion of demographic information. While on written questionnaires, one usually places these questions at the end, we find that answering such questions initially gives psychiatric patients an immediate success experience. These questions are non-threatening, familiar, and factual. As anxiety about the interview is offset by actually doing it, most patients begin to relax. This time also gives the therapist a chance to get a sense of the patient without the stress of having to listen to complex data with an eye toward how to rate the information later. Nevertheless, if you want to adapt this section because of the type of data needed or the style of interviewing, feel free to do so. Remember to have some transition phrase in mind when ending the demographic section and beginning the actual interview. (See Appendix: the Chart Review and Background Information Form.)

The interview questions are designed to address components from the model of human occupation. Although the order of the interview questions is generally consistent with how the components are presented in the theoretical material, there are several exceptions. In order to start the interview in a non-threatening manner, the first question is about *interests* rather than *personal causation* and *values/goals*. Each of these components is part of the volition subsystem. These questions seem to follow naturally at the end of the interview, so they are addressed at that point. Similarly, questions about the past are often painful to psychiatric patients; therefore, they are asked in the middle of the interview after a greater degree of rapport and trust is established between the patient and the interviewer.

Interests
- How do you like to spend your time?
- Do you have any other special interests?
- How often do you participate?

Roles
- When people ask you what you do, what do you tell them?
- What kind of responsibilities do you have as a _____?
  (Fill in "role" from previous response or from demographic information obtained earlier.)

Habits
- Do you generally have a daily schedule that lets you do the things you need to do and want to do?
- Tell me what it is like.
- Over the past six months to a year, has there been a change in how you spend your time?

(If yes...) What is the change and how do you feel about it?

Skills
- In your daily activities, what things do you know how to do well?
  — How well do you feel you get along with people?
  — How about making decisions and solving problems?
  — Do you have any physical limitations or anything that keeps you from doing activities you want to do?
- In order to do the activities you are interested in, are there any skills you feel you need to improve or want to learn?

Output
- Overall, how satisfied are you with how you spend your time?
- Do you feel your daily routine allows you to use your skills to the best of your ability?

- Are there things you would like to do but you do not get a chance?

Physical Environment

- Are there any activities you do not participate in because you do not have enough money?
  - Or transportation to get there?
  - Or there are not facilities in your home or neighborhood?

Social Environment

- Who are the most important people in your life right now?
- What do they think you ought to do?
- Do you agree with them?

Feedback

- How do you know when it is time for you to make a change?
- Are there things or people that affect your making a change?
- How do you use information or feedback from others to make changes?

Historical

- Overall, do you feel you have had the usual ups and downs or do you feel your past has been exceptionally better or worse than that?
- What are some examples of when you were doing the best?
- How old were you during your worst times? What was going on then?

Personal Causation

- What accomplishments, skills, or talents are you most proud of?
- Are there any activities you do in which you lack confidence or feel unsuccessful?
- Have you taken any steps toward developing your skills or confidence in this area?
- Over the next few months, how successful do you think you will be?

Values and Goals

- What things are most important for you, or do you value in your life?
- What are your goals?
- What are your plans for the next few weeks?
- What do you see yourself doing one year from now?
- What do you see yourself doing 5 to 10 years from now?
- What have you worked on in the hospital that you feel will help you meet these goals?

Now let us look at the intent of each group of questions in terms of how they relate to the case analysis method for the model of human occupation as well as the rating scale guidelines. The purpose of Table 4.1 is twofold: 1) To help understand the relationship between the interview questions and its theoretical base and 2) To clarify the way the interview data will be assessed. The second goal will help the interviewer adapt questions and probe further for the type of data required to make the rating.

The rating scale was developed based on the types of responses that were typical of the patients in the short-term setting in which the instrument was tested. They were revised after the research study to reflect the actual answers to the specific questions. Thus, even though they are numerical, they are primarily descriptive and qualitative in nature.

Those of you familiar with the case analysis method will realize that *feedback* is different from primary Question 10 which is: Does the social environment support successful occupational behavior? This change was made because on the first research study of the instrument, answers to the questions were too abstract to make the rating. The primary question was changed to reflect the change in concept.

Also, *historical* is not included in the case analysis method primary questions, but in the system analysis. It is added here because it makes sense to ask the questions at this point in the interview. Later, the information is analyzed under the system analysis section.

Table 4.1

Relation of Interview to Theoretical Base and Assessment Guidelines

Model Component Definition and Primary Question from the Case Analysis Method	Interview Questions	Assessment of Data: Rating Scale Guidelines
Personal Causation The collection of beliefs and expectations a person holds about his effectiveness in the environment. *Does the individual anticipate successful outcomes of action?*	• What accomplishments, skills, or talents are you most proud of? • Are there any activities you do in which you lack confidence or feel unsuccessful? • Have you taken any steps toward developing your skills or confidence in this area? • Over the next few months, how successful do you think you will be?	**Yield:** To determine current and anticipated view of outcomes. **Probe for:** Number of skills proud of, number of items improving, and degree of anticipation of success.
Values and Goals Images of what is good, right, and/or important for occupational activities or personal accomplishment. *Does the individual have values and goals?*	• What things are most important for you, or do you value in your life? • What are your goals? • What are your plans for the next few weeks? • What do you see yourself doing one year from now? • What do you see yourself doing 5 to 10 years from now? • What have you worked on in the hospital that you feel will help you meet these goals?	**Yield:** To determine relatedness between values and goals over time. **Probe for:** Number of plans and their relevance to identified values and goals.
Interests Experience of pleasure in occupations, leisure or work related. *Does the individual have interests?*	• How do you like to spend your time? • Do you have any other special interests? • How often do you participate?	**Yield:** To identify interests and frequency of participation. **Probe for:** Amount/variety (four or more) and frequency (regularly pursued)
Roles Self image of occupying positions in social groups and one's expectations about the obligations of that role. May be a worker, student, parent, home maintainer, participant in an organization, etc. *Does the individual have a primary occupational role?*	• When people ask you what you do, what do you tell them? • What kind of responsibilities do you have as a _____? (Fill in "role" from previous response or from demographic information obtained earlier.)	**Yield:** To identify activities of one role, in detail. **Probe for:** Activities (five or more) of primary role and extent to which they are realistically and specifically described. Remember, this is a screening interview so only a primary role is necessary to identify. Follow-up interviews may seek to explore other roles if necessary. Be sure to count number of activities interviewee identifies as part of his primary role. If you are unfamiliar with role, ask patient for more clarification so that you can determine the extent to which the explanation is realistic.

Table 4.1
Relation of Interview to Theoretical Base and Assessment Guidelines (Concluded)

Model Component Definition and Primary Question from the Case Analysis Method	Interview Questions	Assessment of Data: Rating Scale Guidelines
Habits Images of the routine and typical ways a person performs. Emphasis here is on degree of organization. *Does the individual have organized habit patterns?*	• Do you generally have a daily schedule that lets you do the things you need to do and want to do? • Tell me what it is like. • Over the past 6 months to a year, has there been a change in how you spend your time? (If yes...) What is the change and how do you feel about it?	Yield: To determine degree of organization of daily schedule. Probe for: Balance among work, leisure, and self-maintenance activities. Clarify difference between days and evenings, weekdays with weekend. Listen to manner in which reports daily activities, amount of activities, and exclusion of work or leisure.
Skills Abilities for the production of various forms of purposeful behavior. *Does the individual have performance skills to carry out valued activities?*	• In your daily activities, what things do you know how to do well? — How well do you feel you get along with people? — How about making decisions and solving problems? — Do you have any physical limitations or anything that keeps you from doing activities you want to do? • In order to do the activities you are interested in, are there any skills you feel you need to improve or want to learn?	Yield: To determine assessment of strengths and weaknesses with regard to skills. Constituents of skills (process, motor, and interactional/communication). Listen for areas of satisfaction and competence. Compare with the degree to which skill level in particular activities limits enjoyment or performance.
Output Occupational behavior as an overt expression of the patterns of internal organization within the human system. *Does the individual use performance skills competently and consistently?*	• Overall, how satisfied are you with how you spend your time? • Do you feel your daily routine allows you to use your skills to the best of your ability? • Are there things you would like to do but you do not get a chance?	Yield: To determine degree of satisfaction with time and level of active involvement. Probe for: Degree to which integrates skills and routines into competent and satisfying occupational behavior. Listen for balance between work and leisure. This differs from previous question on level of skills; this asks does he use the skills he has.
Physical Environment External factors with which the individual interacts, such as space, objects, money, transportation, etc. *Does the physical environment support the use of skills?*	• Are there any activities you do not participate in because you do not have enough money? — Or transportation to get there? — Or there are not facilities in your home or neighborhood?	Yield: To determine effect on performance of valued activities. Probe for: Number of problems mentioned and extent of consequences on performance.

Social Environment

People with whom the individual interacts, such as parents, bosses, spouse, co-workers, family members, friends, etc.

Does the social environment require roles that the individual enjoys and performs well?

- Who are the most important people in your life right now?
- What do they think you ought to do?
- Do you agree with them?

Yield: To determine views of important people regarding major goals or issues.

Probe for: Values and attitudes of significant others about individual's role performance. Listen for extent of agreement on specific goals compared with general support. Determine if attitudes are mostly advice giving or if there is little involvement in the individual's life.

Feedback

Information to the individual about the process and consequences of actions.

Does the individual use feedback to support adaptive change?

- How do you know when it is time for you to make a change?
- Are there things or people that affect your making a change?
- How do you use information or feedback from others to make changes?

Yield: To determine extent to which individual uses feedback to reorganize behavior.

Probe for: Extent to which individual seeks support from others or seeks advice. Listen for extent and nature of changes made. Listen for degree of self-reflection used to think about and make changes.

Historical

The functioning and experiences of the individual over time.

How has the individual perceived past performance?

- Overall, do you feel you have had the usual ups and downs or do you feel your past has been exceptionally better or worse than that?
- What are some examples of when you were doing the best?
- How old were you during your worst times? What was going on then?

Yield: To determine perception of pattern of past functioning.

Probe for: Length of time doing well and when that was. Also extent and number of examples of times when doing poorly.

Modifying the Interview

Now that you have seen the relationships among the theoretical framework, the intent of the interview questions, and the criteria for clinical assessment, you are ready to try the interview. You may wish to listen to the audiotape first to hear how the interview flows and the types of responses it elicits.

Then, after trying it several times in your setting, you may wish to change some of the interview questions to better address the levels of functioning of your patients or to suit your personal style of phrasing questions. The chart below provides a way to make changes consistently. If you are in a department with other occupational therapists, the chart gives a format for focusing on specific suggestions and recording them so that the interviewers can learn from one another. You may also wish to note transition statements in the second and third columns. (See Table 4.2)

References

1. Kielhofner, G. and Henry, A. (1988), "Development and investigation of the occupational performance history interview," *American Journal of Occupational Therapy*, 42:489-498.

2. Mishler, E. (1986), *Research Interviewing: Context and Narrative*, Cambridge, MA: Harvard University Press.

Table 4.2
Modifying the Interview

Interview Questions	Problems with Questions and Rationale for Changes	Suggested Replacements for Interview Questions
Personal Causation		
• What accomplishments, skills, or talents are you most proud of?		
• Are there any activities you do in which you lack confidence or feel unsuccessful?		
• Have you taken any steps toward developing your skills or confidence in this area?		
• Over the next few months, how successful do you think you will be?		
Values and Goals		
• What things are most important for you, or do you value in your life?	For patients early in hospital stay, reword.	What would you like to work on in the hospital that you feel will help you meet these goals?
• What are your goals?	For some patients, the idea of goals is too abstract.	What do you think you need to work out or improve in to function better at home?
• What are your plans for the next few weeks?		
• What do you see yourself doing one year from now?		
• What do you see yourself doing 5 to 10 years from now?		
• What have you worked on in the hospital that you feel will help you meet these goals?		
Interests		
• How do you like to spend your time?	Need transition statement from demographic information to interview.	_____, let's switch gears. (Patient's name)
• Do you have any other special interests?	Some patients have a good "play" history, but do not value it enough to talk about it.	Have you had any interests in the past that you don't any longer?
• How often do you participate?		

Table 4.2
Modifying the Interview (Concluded)

Interview Questions	Problems with Questions and Rationale for Changes	Suggested Replacements for Interview Questions
Roles		
• When people ask you what you do, what do you tell them? • What kind of responsibilities do you have as a _____? (Fill in "role" from previous response or from demographic information obtained earlier.)	Patients have had difficulty understanding questions as stated. It is difficult to get a sense of role balance from these questions.	What is your main role in life? What kind of responsibilities do you have in this role? What are your three most important roles?
Habits		
• Do you generally have a daily schedule that lets you do the things you need to do and want to do? • Tell me what it is like. • Over the past 6 months to a year, has there been a change in how you spend your time? (If yes...) What is the change and how do you feel about it?		
Skills		
• In your daily activities, what things do you know how to do well? — How well do you feel you get along with people? — How about making decisions and solving problems? — Do you have any physical limitations or anything that keeps you from doing activities you want to do? • In order to do the activities you are interested in, are there any skills you feel you need to improve or want to learn?	These questions do not address planning skill.	How are you at planning, i.e., your time, activities, and on the job?

Output • Overall, how satisfied are you with how you spend your time? • Do you feel your daily routine allows you to use your skills to the best of your ability? • Are there things you would like to do but you do not get a chance?	Phrase "daily routine" may confuse a therapist learning the model of human occupation with the definition of habits.	Do you feel you have the opportunity to use your skills to the best of your ability?
Physical Environment • Are there any activities you do not participate in because you do not have enough money? — Or transportation to get there? — Or there are not facilities in your home or neighborhood?		
Social Environment • Who are the most important people in your life right now? • What do they think you ought to do? • Do you agree with them?	Patients have difficulty knowing what to answer.	Do you ever seek advice or guidance from them? Do you agree with their opinion or input? How supportive are they in regard to your lifestyle and personal goals?
Feedback • How do you know when it is time for you to make a change? • Are there things or people that affect your making a change? • How do you use information or feedback from others to make changes?	Questions are awkward for therapist's style and patients need more clues to know what this means.	How do you know when it is time for you to make a change? (pause) For instance, do you listen to your feelings or listen to what others say? Are there things or people that affect your making a change? How do you use the advice or feedback from others to make changes?
Historical • Overall, do you feel you have had the usual ups and downs or do you feel your past has been exceptionally better or worse than that? • What are some examples of when you were doing the best? • How old were you during your worst times? What was going on then?		

Chapter Five
Making the Ratings

Use of the Rating Scale

After the interview, compare the interviewee's responses with the intent of the question (the primary analytic question and the yield), then read the rating scale for that variable starting with the first descriptor, rating 5. Notice the criteria for making the ratings for each level. Make sure you understand the differing characteristics for each of the five levels. Think about which of the descriptors best describes the patient's response.

The rating scale is ordinal, which means the possible responses are rank ordered along a single dimension continuum. This is not to be confused with interval level data, which looks similar but assumes that the distance between each of the ratings is equal. Likert scales are an example in which the ratings range from strongly agree to strongly disagree with the middle range being neutral. The advantage of interval data is that more statistical tests can be used to evaluate the findings. However, this was not used for the OCAIRS because an effort was made to increase the stability of ratings by different raters. This was attempted by describing what each of the levels means in terms of behavior.

The disadvantage of this approach is that the rating is more complex than making a consistent rating of 5 through 1 for each question. The rater cannot assume with the OCAIRS that a 3 on *interests* is equivalent to a 3 on *personal causation*. Nor can the rater assume the difference between each rating of a variable is equivalent. The ordinal levels only show a range of responses along a continuum for each variable.

The reasons for this approach are:

1. *To objectify clinical judgment.*
   By using descriptors rather than numbers and a subjective evaluation of degree of agreement with a statement, the rating is more objective.
2. *To create a profile of the patient based on qualitative data.*
   By describing behavior in each area, a richer picture of the patient emerges than would by using numbers alone. Qualitative data matches the clinical situation and the experience of therapists who are accustomed to making interpretations based on multiple observations and interviews with patients in a variety of settings.
3. *To enable a determination of reliability of the measure through quantitative data.*
   By using a rating scale, numbers can be added and statistically compared for each case and by each rater.

Keep in mind the ratings were developed from actual observations of patients over time in a short-term inpatient psychiatric clinical setting. This is characteristic of qualitative research in which the hypotheses derive from the actual data. In this case the rating levels are like hypotheses about how various psychiatric patients respond to questions about their self-perception in occupational tasks and roles. Inductive reasoning was used to make sense of behavior, try a scheme for categorizing responses, observe some more, refine the ratings, pilot test the instrument, revise again, and so on.

Since instrument development is truly an ongoing process, if you consistently have problems making a rating on a certain variable, please notify us about what the problem is and give us suggestions for solutions. These can be incorporated in future revisions and are crucial to making an instrument that has clinical utility.

Meanwhile, most of the time, you should be able to make a decision based on the descriptor given. If not, use the more subjective approach of considering 5 as very adaptive, 3 as average, and 1 as very maladaptive. Also remember that there really is no "right" answer for each variable. Inter-rater reliability, for example, is based on a correlation among the various raters. There is not an assumption of a perfect correlation. Raters can vary on several items by one or two points and still have a relatively stable rating for the instrument as a whole.

Guidelines for Rating Each Component

Personal Causation

5   Expresses much confidence about abilities and anticipates very successful outcomes of action. Identifies at least three skills proud of, states at least one item is improving, and indicates that anticipates success.

4   Expresses pretty much confidence about abilities and anticipates pretty successful outcomes of action. Identifies one or two skills proud of, states at least one step taken to improve, and indicates that anticipates being somewhat successful.

3   Expresses some confidence about abilities and anticipates somewhat successful outcomes of action. Identifies one or two skills, no areas or steps taken to improve, and indicates that anticipates being mostly unsuccessful or lists no areas of unsuccessful performance and is overly confident about skills.

2   Expresses little confidence about abilities and anticipates barely successful outcomes of action. Does not identify anything to be proud of and indicates that anticipates being unsuccessful.

1   Does not express feelings about abilities or outcomes.

The main difficulty here is between a rating of 3 and 4. A patient may sound and look depressed, so you would see them as having only some confidence about their abilities (rating of 3), but they say they expect to be pretty successful and can list at least one step they have taken to improve. Therefore, you give them a rating of 4.

This is an example of how the rating scale is inconsistent in the subjective meaning of each numerical rating, rather it describes a profile of the individual. If you use the recording form in your medical chart, you should remind the staff that although this evaluation gives quantitative data, they should pay more attention to the qualitative data given in the comments section of each variable.

Values and Goals

5 Identifies a variety (three or more) plans for the next few weeks. The plans are consistent with patient's values and long-term goals.

4 Identifies a few (one or two) plans. The plans are consistent with values and goals.

3 Identifies a few (one or two of each) related values and plans, but may not mention any goals or may not be consistent with goal(s).

2 Identifies no or vague plans, a few unrelated values, and vague goals.

1 Does not identify any goals, may have a vague plan.

Rating includes amount of and relatedness among several factors — goals, plans (i.e., short-term goals), and long-term goals. For example, an individual who receives a rating of 3 may report a goal to keep a job, a value of family life, and a plan to relax, go to the beach, and just have fun for a while. The number of plans exceeds one or two, but the thrust of the plan is to avoid working towards goal at this time. It is not clear if vacation plan included being with family (a value) — this should have been clarified during the interview.

Interests

5 Identifies a variety (four or more) of satisfying interests; two activities pursued regularly.

4 Identifies a variety (four or more) of satisfying interests; participation is variable.

3 Identifies a few (one to three) interests; one activity pursued regularly.

2 Identifies a few (one to three) interests; no particular activity is pursued on a regular basis.

1 Does not identify any interests.

This question involves two parts; variety and frequency of participation. Variety is defined in parentheses and quantitatively. Frequency is a judgment call. For example, jogging three times a week is regular, as is bowling once a week. However, because jogging is an aerobic activity, doing it once a week is considered variable participation. Bowling, which is a year-round activity, is considered variable if a person says he does it whenever he feels like it.

Analyzing the differences among the ratings for this variable is like using a decision tree. First decide if the person identifies a variety of interests (four or more) or a few (three or less). Then decide if participation is regular (receiving a rating of 5 if there was also a variety of interests or a 4 if the participation was variable). Few interests makes the choice a rating of 3 or 2 — use the participation amount to decide. If no interests are listed, for whatever reason (resistance, depression, lack of interest), rate a 1.

It takes practice to listen to the responses and not take off points for symptomatology. Do not routinely rate a patient lower because it takes a long time to answer (e.g., a depressed mood) or the answer is concrete, tangential, or any other symptom. Some of the variables do ask that you consider how they organize their response and the pathology is noted there. However, the purpose of this instrument is to assess the degree of adaptive occupational behavior. This is often in spite of or in addition to a psychiatric illness. Therefore, the patient should be primarily viewed for his perception of performance.

Roles

5   Realistically describes many (five or more) activities or obligations of a primary role.

4   Realistically describes several (three to four) activities or obligations of a primary role.

3   Realistically describes one or two activities or obligations of a primary role.

2   Somewhat realistically (or vaguely) describes the activities or obligations of a primary role.

1   Does not describe a primary role.

The main factor requiring clinical judgment is the extent to which the response is realistic. Then count the number of activities described to determine the patient's sense of what is required to perform the role.

Habits

5   Describes a very well-organized daily schedule of valued activities. There is a balance among work, leisure, and self-maintenance activities.

4   Describes a pretty well-organized daily schedule of valued activities. However, there are either no leisure or no work activities mentioned.

3   Describes a somewhat well-organized daily schedule of activities (not necessarily valued). The report is somewhat disjointed.

2   Describes a minimally organized daily schedule of activities. The person does not do very much in a day.

1   Does not describe a daily schedule of activities.

Reflect on the detail in describing the day. Look for type of activities, balance among them, and amount of activity. The way in which the report is given, as well as its content, is important. The descriptors are fairly straightforward.

Skills

5   Has adequate skills for all of current and projected activities. Mostly wants to improve skills to increase already competent and enjoyable activities.

4   Has adequate skills for most of current and projected activities. However, to be satisfied in leisure or work would need to learn some new skill(s).

3   Has adequate skills for some of current and projected activities. However, level of skills limit optimal performance. Manner of responding is rather global (vague) or too focused (concrete).

2   Has adequate skills for few of current and projected activities. Level of skills impedes ability to work or have a productive role. Response may not totally make sense.

1   Does not identify skills.

This question requires substantial knowledge and skill on the part of the rater to make an appropriate rating. First, the rater must be familiar with analyzing activities into their constituents of skills. According to the model of human occupation (and compared with uniform terminology) these are: process skills (cognitive functions such as planning, decision making, and problem solving), motor skills (sensory motor and sensory integrative), and interpersonal/communication (social and psychological components).

Second, the rater must be familiar with the demographic information about the patient's recent history. For instance, think about the reason for admission, functioning over the past year, and presenting symptoms.

Finally, compare the patient's perception of his skills with his responses on each of the preceding questions (interests, roles, and habits).

The reason this question is more complicated to think through is that the patient's pathology may be interfering with his response to this question. For instance, concrete thinking, grandiosity, vagueness, or tangential responses are evidence of process skill dysfunction even if the patient's perception of his skills is that they are adequate. Therefore, the rating of 3 and 2 may reflect skills as reported or reflect a thought or mood disorder affecting thoughts, movements, and interactions. So far you have rated interests based on your sense of how active and satisfied the patient is in how he spends his time.

You have rated roles for the extent to which the person can identify a primary role and realistically explain the responsibilities of that role. You have rated habits on how organized the patient's description of his schedule appears to be. Now you are rating the adequacy of skills for the activities the patient performs and intends to perform. Your position relative to the information is the same, the difference is that you look beyond the one variable for your data and you use more theory to interpret the meaning.

Output

5 Integrates all of skills and routines into competent and satisfying occupational behavior. Participates in work and leisure activities.

4 Integrates most of skills and routines into competent and somewhat satisfying behavior. Patient works but does not participate in leisure activities.

3 Integrates some of skills and routines into competent behavior, but may not be satisfied. Either works or is involved in leisure, but not both.

2 Integrates few of skills and routines into competent or satisfying occupational behavior. Usually is not satisfied and not using skills.

1 Does not report degree of satisfaction with occupational behavior.

Rating is based on how well the person routinely engages in occupational behavior as well as the degree of satisfaction reported. This assesses quality of life and quantity of occupation. Rating 4 is typical of workaholics. Rating 2 indicates an absence of a productive role allowing integration of skills and routines.

Physical Environment

5 Physical environment supports the performance of valued activities very well. No problems mentioned.

4 Physical environment supports the performance of valued activities pretty well. One problem mentioned.

3 Physical environment supports the performance of valued activities to some extent. Two problems mentioned.

2 Physical environment supports the performance of valued activities very poorly. Problems have a major consequence (e.g., cannot make ends meet).

1 Does not describe physical environment or says that there are no problems in a resistant/non-cooperative manner.

Descriptors are self explanatory. Note that what is rated is patient's perception of the environment. For this reason, it is important to check out the actual availability of community resources or compare the individual's perceptions with a family member's.

Social Environment

5 Values and attitudes of significant others support successful role performance very much. Comments reflect active support of patient's goals and some collaboration in daily life.

4 Values and attitudes of significant others support successful role performance pretty much. Comments reflect general support of patient and less involvement in daily life.

3 Values and attitudes of significant others support successful role performance somewhat. Attitude is mostly judgmental and advice giving (e.g., mostly "shoulds").

2 Values and attitudes of significant others support successful role performance very little. There is lack of interest in and involvement with the patient.

1 Does not identify values and attitudes.

Difficulty arises for the rater when the patient has few goals and is involved in a self-destructive or at least unsuccessful lifestyle. Then the significant others may be giving advice (rating of 3) which is supportive (rating of 4 or 5) of a higher level of functioning. However, the patient may not see it as supportive because he is denying the extent of his problems or is too depressed to evaluate the situation accurately. In this case, rate the variable from the patient's perspective, e.g., 3., because the patient does not see his social supports as supportive even if you think they are or have potential to be. Your sense of this situation can be reflected later in the system analysis, the contextual rating.

Feedback

5 Uses feedback to make adaptive changes very well. Patient seeks support from others and makes adaptive changes.

4 Uses feedback to make adaptive changes pretty well. Patient seeks advice from others and makes some changes, although less consistently adaptive.

3 Uses feedback to make adaptive changes to some extent. Patient demonstrates some self-reflection but only makes a few changes.

2 Uses feedback to make adaptive changes minimally. Patient demonstrates little self-reflection and is largely unsuccessful in making changes.

1 Does not describe the use of feedback.

Make this rating based on all the information collected so far — from history of illness based on chart review and background information and any of the interview questions covered. Consider whether there were any indications of the patient having made changes or being involved in using feedback. Add this information to the response given for this variable. The rating includes the type of feedback as well as the nature of the changes.

The assumption is that a person who is well adjusted uses both internal and external feedback. Since "support" on the previous question about significant others in the social environment is considered a higher rating than "advice," then to be consistent an individual who seeks "support" as a form of feedback receives a higher rating than one who seeks "advice." This is because using support may reflect a greater sense of one's self in evaluating the feedback from others than seeking advice might if done in a needy, dependent, or unintegrated manner.

A rating of 3 indicates the individual is not involved with others for feedback. Although the descriptor may sound more self-reliant, it is assumed there is less feedback at this level to integrate. The self-reflection is in isolation compared with a rating of 4 or 5 in which self-reflection is in the context of input from relationships. A rating of 2 reflects little self-awareness or introspection.

In terms of degree of adaptive change, a rating of 5 reflects a history of adaptive changes. A rating of 4 reflects less consistently adaptive changes. A rating of 3 means the patient may not have cited any examples of change except for coming to the hospital when in need of help. A rating of 2 reflects the patient is largely unsuccessful when making changes.

Historical

5 Perceives all of past functioning as adaptive. Patient has been doing well for a long time, no real low points aside from the usual ups and downs.

4 Perceives most of past functioning as adaptive. Patient has been doing well for a long time but currently has a problem. May identify one example of a worst time which the individual perceives as traumatic.

3 Perceives some of past functioning as adaptive. Patient is currently having difficulty and cites several examples of problematic times in the past.

2 Perceives little of past functioning as adaptive. Patient has been having difficulty for a long time fairly consistently. Patient does not mention any examples of past good times and has no productive role currently.

1 Does not identify how he perceives past functioning.

Rate individual's self perception about past performance in comparison with responses on interview up to and including this question. This will help round out the response if the patient does not elaborate fully. If you find discrepancies between how you see the patient and how he sees himself, make the rating based on the patient's self-perception, but note the discrepancy on the recording form by the space for historical information in the system analysis section.

Making the System Analysis Ratings

The *system analysis* involves four ratings grounded in the general systems theory on which the model of human occupation is based. The ratings you make bring to life the systems adage, "the whole is greater than the sum of its parts." In the previous ratings, you analyzed each component of the system separately. This helps give you an idea of how the patient is functioning in each specific area. Now, the system's rating requires that you integrate all these elements to answer more holistic questions. These questions are as follows: How are all these various parts interacting to affect the whole person?; How did this person get the way he is?; Where is he headed?; and How does his environment influence him? As you can imagine, this is one of the hardest parts of the instrument requiring the most experience and understanding of systems theory. But, it is also most important that your picture of the patient is an integrated, not fragmented, one. The following sections discuss these ratings, and Table 5.1 provides additional guidelines for the ratings and the systems analysis rating scale.

Dynamic Rating

The *dynamic* rating addresses the gestalt functioning of the individual. Some examples for the dynamic rating might help make this more clear. If a patient tells you that she is fatalistic about her chances of making friends and also reports that she is shy and feels uncomfortable around others, you have evidence of negative synergy. That is, she has weak communication skills, which are making it difficult for her to feel confident. Another example is a patient who reports that he has the goal to achieve a college degree — that could be a real strength. But, if he reports poor study habits, the goal is probably unrealistic. If he has good study habits, the goal is adaptive because it is likely to be reached. These two examples illustrate that the dynamic rating reflects how the various elements of the system interact to determine adaptation.

Historical Rating

The *historical* rating considers the impact of the person's life experiences over time. A person who was functional at one time is likely to have a better chance of adapting in the future than someone who has never functioned well. A person who failed at a particular kind of performance is likely to avoid that performance in the future. Each person's history influences his present. The historical rating asks you: How is this person's past influencing his present?

Contextual Rating

The third rating is *contextual*. It refers to the interaction of the person with the environment. The contextual rating answers the questions: How is the environment influencing this person's adaptation? How well is this person satisfying the demands of his or her environment?

System Trajectory

The last rating is the *system trajectory*. The concept of trajectory refers to where the person is headed. This assessment is the most comprehensive of all the ratings, for it builds on the previous three system analyses — dynamic, historical, and contextual. This is where you make a predictive rating — a prognosis. You could make a graph of this (Figure 5.1). If he has been doing well, continues to function adaptively, and you would predict will continue to be effective without any need for your intervention, you would show a straight line or a line going up slightly.

If the patient has been doing okay but is at risk to go downhill, you could show the dip in function and the downhill slope that is likely to occur unless occupational therapy intervenes (and other parts of the treatment program as well).

When you get to this point in the evaluation, you are ready to identify treatment goals or discharge goals to discuss with the patient and the patient's team. A treatment or discharge plan should follow based on the realities of your program and setting, the desires of the patient, and the support and opportunities in the patient's environment.

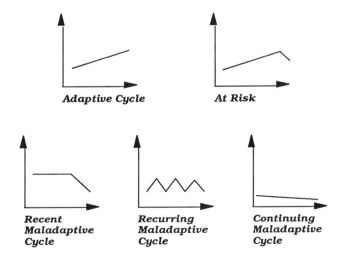

Adaptive Cycle   *At Risk*

Recent Maladaptive Cycle   *Recurring Maladaptive Cycle*   *Continuing Maladaptive Cycle*

Figure 5.1
System Trajectories

Table 5.1
Relation of System Analysis to Assessment Guidelines and Rating Scale

Model Components Definitions and System Analysis Global Assessments	Assessment of Data: Rating Scale Guidelines	Rating Scale for System Analysis
Dynamic The ongoing interactive status of the system. *How do the individual's system elements work together?*	Compare responses (not only ratings) to questions dealing with throughput. For example, compare the volitional subsystem with output. The volitional subsystem includes responses to personal causation, values/goals, and interests. The output assumes use of role performance, routine habits, and level of skills to achieve competence and feel satisfaction. Write a description of how these aspects of the individual's functioning to determine how they interact with each other.	**5** Individual's output is competent and consistent with volitional subsystem. The individual performs valued activities well. **4** Individual's output is moderate and consistent with volitional subsystem. The individual has fairly realistic goals for his moderate level of skills and ability to deal with obstacles. **3** Individual's output is inconsistent with volitional subsystem or has minimal output and volition. The individual has unrealistically high or low expectations compared with skills. **2** Individual's output is incompetent and consistent with volitional subsystem. The individual does not identify realistic plans or a desire to change. Performance is very limited. **1** Unable to determine to what extent the throughput elements interact consistently.
Historical The functioning and experiences of the individual over time. *How has the individual perceived past performance?*	Determine perception of pattern of past functioning. Consider length of time doing well and when that was. Also extent and number of examples of times when doing poorly.	**5** Perceives all of past functioning as adaptive. Patient has been doing well for a long time, no real low points aside from the usual ups and downs. **4** Perceives most of past functioning as adaptive. Patient has been doing well for a long time but currently has a problem. May identify one example of worst time, which the individual perceives as traumatic. **3** Perceives some of past functioning as adaptive. Patient is currently having difficulty and cites several examples of problematic times in the past.

2 Perceives little of past functioning as adaptive. Patient has been having difficulty for a long time fairly consistently. Patient does not mention any examples of past good times and has no productive role currently.

1 Does not identify how perceives past functioning.

Contextual

The conditions in the environment and how they are brought to bear on the system.

How does the individual appear to function in the usual environment?

Compare responses (not only ratings) from dynamic assessment (above) to physical and social environment and use of feedback.

Think about how the individual's abilities and actions are supported by his or her community, work or home situation, and significant relationships. Consider what bearing the individual's use of feedback has on his ability to adapt to and function effectively in his current environment.

5 Individual's output and volitional subsystem are very congruent with factors present in the usual environment.

4 Individual's output and volitional subsystem are pretty congruent with factors present in the usual environment.

3 Individual's output and volitional subsystem are somewhat congruent with factors present in the usual environment.

2 Individual's output and volitional subsystem are minimally congruent with factors present in the usual environment.

1 Unable to determine to what extent these factors are congruent with the present environment.

System Trajectory

The overall pattern of the system.

What is the tendency toward an adaptive or maladaptive cycle?

Compare the responses from the historical, dynamic, and contextual system analyses to make a prediction about the system trajectory. Based on your clinical experience and assessment of how the many factors interact with each other in this individual's life, identify to what extent the individual is in an adaptive or maladaptive cycle. Link this assessment to need for occupational therapy services.

5 Currently in an adaptive cycle and is expected to continue without occupational therapy services.

4 At risk to enter a maladaptive cycle and needs occupational therapy to assess maintenance of organized behavior.

3 Currently in a recent maladaptive cycle and needs occupational therapy services to reorganize.

2 Currently in a recurring maladaptive cycle and needs occupational therapy services to reorganize and prevent reoccurrence.

1 Currently in a continuing maladaptive cycle and needs occupational therapy services to learn how to organize.

Chapter Six
Completing the Assessment

Recording on the Summary Form

After conducting the interview and making the ratings for each component, the therapist is ready to summarize the findings and begin treatment or discharge planning. The Summary Form (see Appendix) is useful for synthesizing the results of the assessment on one page. The comments section provides the therapist space to indicate the rationale for the numerical ratings and to describe what they mean for this particular patient.

Depending on the setting, the therapist may adapt this form for the patient's chart or summarize the information in a narrative note consistent with the documentation system. Because the terminology is unique to a particular model for occupational therapy, therapists may wish to add definitions of the terms on the summary form or attach an explanatory sheet about the instrument. If the interdisciplinary staff do not understand the form, information will not be effectively communicated.

Full time clinicians often think of research as something that "other" people in the profession do. This is partly because of time constraints in the practice setting and partly because of lack of experience with the research process. But actually, clinicians do research as part of their daily experience when they engage in clinical reasoning[1,2].

Some of the clinical questions therapists have asked about the OCAIRS can be answered by framing the question in terms of research concepts[3,4,5].

1. *If a patient does not offer complete information during the interview, but the information is offered at some other time (for instance, during a treatment group), may I use that information to come up with a rating or must I strictly rate the variable according to what the patient states during the interview?*

   The purpose of having a measurement that has scientific properties is that those using the measure capture accurate and meaningful information. As clinicians, we often collect data first because each new patient presents a different constellation of information, problems, and circumstances.

   Therefore, while using the OCAIRS as the measurement tool, the rater should focus on the information from the interview, but he is not prevented from mentally comparing interview data with other sources of information when making the rating. Because the interview questions and rating scale are an integrated unit, the therapist should get all the basic information needed to do the ratings in the interview, but reference to supporting data is not inappropriate.

2. *If the information given by a patient is inconsistent with the therapist's observation or if the therapist questions the validity of the patient's answer, should that be considered in the rating?*

   This question is related to the previous one in that it has to do with the reliability of the *patient* as a measurement tool. If the patient's self-perception and therefore his self-report is inaccurate, then that needs to be reported and can be considered in the rating scale.

   When rating the OCAIRS, most of the variables should be rated primarily on the patient's self-perception and self-report. However, the system analysis ratings provide the therapist an opportunity to take his observations and opinions into account. Certainly, since the OCAIRS presents a descriptive profile of the patient as well as a quantitative picture, these discrepancies should be noted in the comments and taken into account in treatment and discharge planning.

3. *If a patient does not understand a question (such as under Social Environment "What do they think you ought to do?"), may the therapist elaborate on what they are asking?*

Yes, this issue was addressed in the chapter on the interview, but we can say more about it here. Structured interviews are characterized by strict wording. All probes or restatements are thought out before hand. The intent of these interviews is to be standardized, assuming that whoever does the interview will do it the same way no matter what the circumstances or population.

Unstructured interviews are at the opposite extreme. They are more like a conversation and the questions and answers are unique to the people involved at that particular time and place. These interviews are invaluable to ethnographic research in the field.

The OCAIRS is designed to be more flexible than a standardized interview because of the understanding that each clinical setting differs sufficiently to make the phrasing and meaning of certain questions non-uniform. By the same token, in an effort to maintain reliability and validity of the instrument, it is not as free-form as the unstructured interview.

The research concept that is helpful here is *content validity.* Content validity seeks to determine if the information measured by the instrument is representative of what should be measured. If you change an interview question for further clarification, you have the definitions from the model of human occupation, as reflected in the case analysis method, as your measure of consistency. If a reworded question yields the same concept, there is no problem in changing the question.

4. *We commonly have patients diagnosed as schizoaffective with whom we would like to use the OCAIRS. Is there any reason we cannot use it? Why did your study sample exclude people with that diagnosis?*

When designing the original study of reliability, only two diagnostic groups were selected in order to get "cleaner" results — depression and schizophrenia. We were interested in accounting for differences between the groups should they occur. Research designs always reflect tension between internal validity and external validity. By controlling for as many variables as possible in the design (and enhancing internal validity), the ability to generalize outside the study sample is decreased (affecting the external validity).

Schizoaffective disorder contains aspects of both affective and thought disorders, characteristic of depression and schizophrenia. Since there were no consistent differences between the diagnostic groups in this study, there is no reason to think a patient with a diagnosis of schizoaffective illness would be inappropriate to evaluate. A question that could be posed to address any diagnosis or population not included in the study is: Would you expect the raters to have a more difficult time using the instrument with this group? This is essentially the issue of reliability. If not, use the OCAIRS to evaluate them.

A second relevant question is: Would you expect the interview questions to address issues representative of that population's issues? This was discussed in the first chapter of this manual. The issue here is validity. We cannot assume that the OCAIRS is applicable to adolescents or elderly patients because it may be that their developmental concerns are not reflected adequately in this interview or accurately in the rating scale descriptors. Of course, they might be. We will not know unless research is conducted specifically on these groups or other groups in question, such as prisoners, outpatients recovering from head trauma, or physical rehabilitation patients.

5. *How do I interpret the scores on the rating scale and summary form?*

Most occupational therapy interviews do not include rating scales. One of the most important aspects of the interview process is gathering rich qualitative information about the person. This data is the basis on which you make the ratings and it directly influences your decision-making for intervention. However, the absence of some way to quantify therapists' clinical judgements means we have no way to examine reliability and validity in the classical sense. The addition of the rating scale to the OCAIRS allows us to conduct research with statistical analysis and make some critical comparisons. For example, we can compare the ratings of one therapist with another to determine consistency in making ratings (*inter-rater reliability*).

The scale also gives a shorthand way of representing our clinical judgment. In a very basic sense each rating says, "On a scale of one to five, I consider this person to be a *blank* in terms of adaptiveness in this area." At this stage of assessment development, this is the most we can assert about the rating.

Taken together, the series of ratings gives a *profile* of areas of strength and weakness. This can be a helpful guide in targeting areas for intervention and identifying strengths to enhance with therapy. The quantitative information (the ratings) and the qualitative information provide complimentary data. Making the quantitative ratings forces you to consider what the specific information means in terms of adaptation. The specific qualitative information allows you to think and talk about what the rating means in terms of the individual's life. The ratings tell you how adaptive the person is; the qualitative information gives the necessary information to understand why.

References

1. Rogers, J. (1983), "Clinical reasoning: The ethics, science, and art," *American Journal of Occupational Therapy*, 37:601-616.

2. Schön, D. (1983), *The Reflective Practitioner*, New York: Basic Books.

3. Babbie, E. (1979), *The Practice of Social Research*, (Second ed.) Belmont, CA: Wadsworth.

4. Campbell, D. and Stanley, J. (1963), *Experimental and Quasi-experimental Designs for Research*, Boston: Houghton Mifflin.

5. Cox, R. and West, W. (1986), *Fundamentals of Research for Health Professionals*, (Second ed.) Laurel, MD: RAMSCO.

Chapter Seven
Practicing Using the Instrument

Introduction to the Audiotape

The enclosed audiotape contains two patient interviews using the OCAIRS. In order to maintain patient confidentiality some of the identifying information has been modified and the interviews are role played by two occupational therapists. The interviews are based on videotapes from the study of inter-rater reliability with the post-research version in 1984. The reason videotapes were not included with this manual is that the technical quality was not sufficient. Although the audiotape does not enable viewing nonverbal communication, it provides an opportunity to have more of a feel of the interaction than if the interview was merely written.

The purpose of the interviews is for you to get a chance to hear the flow of the interview and to use the rating scale. You will hear how the interviewer encourages the patient to elaborate, gives feedback, and maintains control of the interview. You will notice the different types of responses from patients with different personalities, problems, and diagnoses.

As you listen, you will probably discover places you would use additional transition statements. You may also be aware of how the patients make you feel during the interviews. Spend time reflecting on this so you can enhance your awareness of transference issues. These personal feelings are always present and it is important to be as conscious as possible of issues that might interfere with the purpose of the interview.

The audiotape is about 20 minutes long on each side. You will hear guitar music to introduce the first side and conclude the second side (a few bars of Bach's Gavotte II played by Kathy Kaplan!). Side A then begins with a brief introduction to the tape and the interview with "Adrianne".

Side B begins with the interview with "Jasmine" and concludes with an informal discussion with three occupational therapists about the two interviews and related issues.

In the next sections of this chapter you will be moving back and forth from the audiotape to the forms and to the manual. You will start by reading the background information on the first case, Adrianne, and then listen to the interview. Next you will make the ratings and then compare your responses with those in the manual. Finally, you will read the comments about the case before repeating the procedure with the second case, Jasmine.

The instructions for the cases are listed at the beginning of each section. The forms that are filled out give you immediate feedback on your ratings and a chance to learn for yourself the thinking behind this case analysis method of assessment. We hope you have fun with this learning process.

Case One: Adrianne

1. Find the following forms in the Appendix and photocopy *two* sets: Occupational Case Analysis Interview and Rating Scale Form, and OCAIRS Summary Form.

2. Read the introduction to *Case One: Adrianne* and the Chart Review and Background Information on page 68.

3. Close the manual and take notes on the interview on the Occupational Case Analysis Interview Rating Scale Form as you listen to the first case, Adrianne, on side one of the audiotape.

4. When the interview is completed, review the data and make the ratings for each area listed on the same form. Refer to Table 4.1 for additional information regarding rating scale guidelines (pages 37–39).

5. Enter your ratings and comments supporting your ratings on the OCAIRS Summary Form. Be alert to recording the ratings in the sequence of the model, not the sequence on the OCAIRS Summary Form.

6. Now return to pages 69–83 in the manual and compare your interview notes, ratings, and summary comments with the handwritten forms. These reflect the assessment of a therapist experienced in using the OCAIRS and allow you an opportunity for self-study.

7. Continue reading about Case One in the *Comments* section for Adrianne, which includes treatment recommendations and issues related to using the instrument with this example (pages 84–86).

Introduction to Adrianne

Adrianne, wearing hospital pajamas and appearing tired, walked slowly to the interview. Her voice was soft and hesitant. She seemed willing to be interviewed due to her previous favorable experience with the inpatient program.

Occupational Case Analysis
Interview and Rating Scale
Chart Review and Background Information Form

Chart Review

Patient Name _Adrianne_

Therapist _____

Team _____

Address _____
_____
_____

Age _34_   Sex _F_   Race _C_

Date of Admission _March 5, 1984_

Diagnosis _Major Repressive Disorder; Substance Abuse-mixed_

Reason for admission, precipitants _to stop feeling like there is nothing to live for, rejected by boyfriend, ETOH → drug detox_

Previous psychiatric history _hospitalized for depression after rape in 1978, treated 1 month_
_____

Condition (mental status, pertinent medical history) _difficulty sleeping, ↓ appetite ↓ interest in work, helpless + hopeless_

Medications _amitriptyline_

Family of origin _father died of cardiac arrest, mother died of cancer_

Background Information

Living situation: House/(apartment)   Own/(rent)

Alone   (With Someone) two children

How long _7 yrs_   Plans to move _I don't know_

Highest grade completed _10_

Classes now (fun, training, self improvement) _no_
_____

Work _Dept of labor - claims clerk_

How long _2 yrs_   Plans to change _I'd like to but no plans yet_

Reason for hospitalization _depressed, drinking_
_____
_____

Interests

- How do you like to spend your time?

  bowl
  movies
  parties

- Do you have any other special interests?

  I don't know

- How often do you participate?

  bowling - every week
  movies + parties - whenever

Rating

5 Identifies a variety (four or more) of satisfying interests; two activities pursued regularly.

4 Identifies a variety (four or more) of satisfying interests; participation is variable.

③ Identifies a few (one to three) interests; one activity pursued regularly.

2 Identifies a few (one to three) interests; no particular activity is pursued on a regular basis.

1 Does not identify any interests.

Roles

- When people ask you what you do, what do you tell them?

  I go to work

- What kind of responsibilities do you have as a <u>*claims clerk*</u> ?

  (Fill in "role" from previous response or from demographic information obtained earlier.)

  count checks
  answer bills
  use computer
  help out in other tasks

Rating

5 Realistically describes many (five or more) activities or obligations of a primary role.

④ Realistically describes several (three to four) activities or obligations of a primary role.

3 Realistically describes one or two activities or obligations of a primary role.

2 Somewhat realistically (or vaguely) describes the activities or obligations of a primary role.

1 Does not describe a primary role.

Habits

- Do you generally have a daily schedule that lets you do the things you need to do and want to do?

  no, not really

- Tell me what it is like.

  get up, go to work, come home cook dinner, look at T.V... get up about 6:00. Before came in - wasn't going to sleep.
  Saturday - groceries, wash clothes, clean house, an activity to do

- Over the past 6 months to a year, has there been a change in how you spend your time?

  (If yes...) What is the change and how do you feel about it?

  going to girlfriend's house getting high, go back home to sleep feels like a bad change

Rating

5 Describes a very well-organized daily schedule of valued activities. There is a balance among work, leisure, and self-maintenance activities.

4 Describes a pretty well-organized daily schedule of valued activities. However, there are either no leisure or no work activities mentioned.

(3) Describes a somewhat well-organized daily schedule of activities (not necessarily valued). The report is somewhat disjointed.

2 Describes a minimally organized daily schedule of activities. The person does not do very much in a day.

1 Does not describe a daily schedule of activities.

Skills

- In your daily activities, what things do you know how to do well?

    I think I do my job good

    — How well do you feel you get along with people?

    no problems at work

    — How about making decisions and solving problems?

    OK

    — Do you have any physical limitations or anything that keeps you from doing activities you want to do?

    no

- In order to do the activities you are interested in, are there any skills you feel you need to improve or want to learn?

    typing

Rating

5 Has adequate skills for all of current and projected activities. Mostly wants to improve skills to increase already competent and enjoyable activities.

4 Has adequate skills for most of current and projected activities. However, to be satisfied in leisure or work would need to learn some new skill(s).

(3) Has adequate skills for some of current and projected activities. However, level of skills limit optimal performance. Manner of responding is rather global (vague) or too focused (concrete).

2 Has adequate skills for few of current and projected activities. Level of skills impedes ability to work or have a productive role. Response may not totally make sense.

1 Does not identify skills.

Output

- Overall, how satisfied are you with how you spend your time?

  I wasn't satisfied. Like to make it different in the world... do more active things - keep from what I was into (drinking)

- Do you feel your daily routine allows you to use your skills to the best of your ability?

  no

- Are there things you would like to do but you do not get a chance?

  plenty, had the time just didn't do it time to sew things, just do different things

Rating

5 Integrates all of skills and routines into competent and satisfying occupational behavior. Participates in work and leisure activities.

4 Integrates most of skills and routines into competent and somewhat satisfying behavior. Patient works but does not participate in leisure activities.

③ Integrates some of skills and routines into competent behavior, but may not be satisfied. Either works or is involved in leisure but not both.

2 Integrates few of skills and routines into competent or satisfying occupational behavior. Usually is not satisfied and not using skills.

1 Does not report degree of satisfaction with occupational behavior.

Physical Environment

- Are there any activities you do not participate in because you do not have enough money?

  money

  — Or transportation to get there?

  —' Or there are not facilities in your home or neighborhood?

  *I'd like to do more exercise
  limited facilities*

Rating

5 Physical environment supports the performance of valued activities very well. No problems mentioned.

4 Physical environment supports the performance of valued activities pretty well. One problem mentioned.

③ Physical environment supports the performance of valued activities to some extent. Two problems mentioned.

2 Physical environment supports the performance of valued activities very poorly. Problems have a major consequence (e.g., cannot make ends meet).

1 Does not describe physical environment or says there are no problems in a resistant/non-cooperative manner.

Social Environment

- Who are the most important people in your life right now?

  my kids (ages 14 & 16)

- What do they think you ought to do?

  you should stop doing that, it's not good for you

- Do you agree with them?

  now yes, at first didn't

Rating

5 Values and attitudes of significant others support successful role performance very much. Comments reflect active support of patient's goals and some collaboration in daily life.

4 Values and attitudes of significant others support successful role performance pretty much. Comments reflect general support of patient and less involvement in daily life.

③ Values and attitudes of significant others support successful role performance somewhat. Attitude is mostly judgmental and advice giving (e.g. mostly "shoulds").

2 Values and attitudes of significant others support successful role performance very little. There is lack of interest in and involvement with the patient.

1 Does not identify values and attitudes.

Feedback

- How do you know when it is time for you to make a change?

  started thinking about harming myself
  felt crazy + silly - came into hospital

- Are there things or people that affect your making a change?

  friends - (observe their routines + habits)

- How do you use information or feedback from others to make changes?

  realized wasn't helping myself
  by drinking, just made it worse

Rating

5 Uses feedback to make adaptive changes very well. Patient seeks support from others and makes adaptive changes.

4 Uses feedback to make adaptive changes pretty well. Patient seeks advice from others and makes some changes, although less consistently adaptive.

③ Uses feedback to make adaptive changes to some extent. Patient demonstrates some self-reflection but only makes a few changes.

2 Uses feedback to make adaptive changes minimally. Patient demonstrates little self-reflection and is largely unsuccessful in making changes.

1 Does not describe the use of feedback.

Historical

- Overall, do you feel you have had the usual ups and downs or do you feel your past has been exceptionally better or worse than that?

  worse, at certain times

- What are some examples of when you were doing the best?

  started doing different jobs at work - doing good then

- How old were you during your worst times? What was going on then?

  childhood & past 4 yrs - same thing (she wouldn't talk about what was happening then)

Rating

5 Perceives all of past functioning as adaptive. Patient has been doing well for a long time, no real low points aside from the usual ups and downs.

4 Perceives most of past functioning as adaptive. Patient has been doing well for a long time but currently has a problem. May identify one example of a worst time which the individual perceives as traumatic.

③ Perceives some of past functioning as adaptive. Patient is currently having difficulty and cites several examples of problematic times in the past.

2 Perceives little of past functioning as adaptive. Patient has been having difficulty for a long time fairly consistently. Patient does not mention any examples of past good times and has no productive role currently.

1 Does not identify how perceives past functioning.

Personal Causation

- What accomplishments, skills, or talents are you most proud of?

  Kept job this long
  way I'm bringing up my children

- Are there any activities you do in which you lack confidence or feel unsuccessful?

  feel I can do something if I want
  to, if I feel like doing it at the time

- Have you taken any steps toward developing your skills or confidence in this area?

  assertiveness

- Over the next few months, how successful do you think you will be?

  try to be very

Rating

5 Expresses much confidence about abilities and anticipates very successful outcomes of action. Identifies at least three skills proud of, states at least one item is improving, and indicates that anticipates success.

④ Expresses pretty much confidence about abilities and anticipates pretty successful outcomes of action. Identifies one or two skills proud of, states at least one step taken to improve, and indicates that anticipates being somewhat successful.

3 Expresses some confidence about abilities and anticipates somewhat successful outcomes of action. Identifies one or two skills, no areas or steps taken to improve, and indicates that anticipates being mostly unsuccessful OR lists no areas of unsuccessful performance and is overly confident about skills.

2 Expresses little confidence about abilities and anticipates barely successful outcomes of action. Does not identify anything to be proud of and indicates that anticipates being unsuccessful.

1 Does not express feelings about abilities or outcomes.

Values and Goals

- What things are most important for you, or do you value, in your life?

  job, children

- What are your goals?

  get out of hospital, deal with problems without crutch, + make life better - move

- What are your plans for the next few weeks?

  go back to work - activities in the evening

- What do you see yourself doing one year from now?

  better job

- What do you see yourself doing 5-10 years from now?

  maybe married by then

- What have you worked on in the hospital that you feel will help you meet these goals? *how not to get angry or depressed exercise to bring out frustration + deal with depression*

I have asked you a lot of questions. Do you have any comments or questions for me?

no

Rating

5 Identifies a variety (three or more) plans for the next few weeks. The plans are consistent with patient's values and long- term goals.

④ Identifies a few (one or two) plans. The plans are consistent with values and goals.

3 Identifies a few (one or two of each) related values and plans, but may not mention any goals or may not be consistent with goal(s).

2 Identifies no or vague plans, a few unrelated values, and vague goals.

1 Does not identify any goals, may have a vague plan.

Dynamic

Compare responses (not only ratings) to questions dealing with throughput. For example, compare the volitional subsystem with output. The volitional subsystem includes responses to personal causation, values/goals, and interests. The output assumes use of role performance, routine habits, and level of skills to achieve competence and feel satisfaction. Write a description of these aspects of the individual's functioning to determine how they interact with each other.

Personal causation - she had difficulty thinking of things she was proud of, did express pride in work + children, confident of future success

Values/Goals - jobs + kids, discuss plans to make changes - move, more activities, no drinking

Interests - Bowl, movies, parties - later exercise + sewing were mentioned

Output - disatisfied with how spends time, had time but just didn't use it. Seems lacking in interpersonal skills - may be affected by dep./work is main focus - doesn't center on activities with kids - whom she says she values.

5 Individual's output is competent and consistent with volitional subsystem. The individual performs valued activities well.

4 Individual's output is moderate and consistent with volitional subsystem. The individual has fairly realistic goals for his or her moderate level of skills and ability to deal with obstacles.

(3) Individual's output is inconsistent with volitional subsystem or has minimal output and volition. The individual has unrealistically high or low expectations compared with skills.

2 Individual's output is incompetent and consistent with volitional subsystem. The individual does not identify realistic plans or a desire to change. Performance is very limited.

1 Unable to determine to what extent the throughput elements interact consistently.

Contextual

Compare responses (not only ratings) from dynamic assessment (above) to physical and social environment and use of feedback. Think about how the individual's abilities and actions are supported by his or her community, work or home situation, and significant relationships. Consider what bearing the individual's use of feedback has on his or her ability to adapt to and function effectively in his or her current environment.

Has some interests + skills. Feels she can make changes if she wants to (denial?). Only mention of friends is in relation to undesired activities. Support system mentioned is 2 teenage kids. States some phys. environ. limitations — money, facilities, no problem stated with time, transportation, or interests.

5 Individual's output and volitional subsystem are very congruent with factors present in the usual environment.

4 Individual's output and volitional subsystem are pretty congruent with factors present in the usual environment.

(3) Individual's output and volitional subsystem are somewhat congruent with factors present in the usual environment.

2 Individual's output and volitional subsystem are minimally congruent with factors present in the usual environment.

1 Unable to determine to what extent these factors are congruent with the present environment.

System Trajectory

Compare the responses from the historical, dynamic, and contextual system analyses to make a prediction about the system trajectory. Based on your clinical experience and assessment of how the many factors interact with each other in this individual's life, identify to what extent the individual is in an adaptive or maladaptive cycle. Link this assessment to need for occupational therapy services.

Describes history as worse than average person. Although she has plans + goals, they seem unrealistic given limited social support system + history of recurrent problems. Plans are not concrete enough to expect follow through without support. Ongoing O.T. (day tx or outpt?) would help promote adaptation.

5 Currently in an adaptive cycle and is expected to continue without occupational therapy services.

4 At risk to enter a maladaptive cycle and needs occupational therapy to assess maintenance of organized behavior.

3 Currently in a recent maladaptive cycle and needs occupational therapy services to reorganize.

(2) Currently in a recurring maladaptive cycle and needs occupational therapy services to reorganize and prevent reoccurrence.

1 Currently in a continuing maladaptive cycle and needs occupational therapy services to learn how to organize.

Occupational Case Analysis
Interview and Rating Scale
Summary Form

Patient _Adrianne_   O.T. Rater _KK_   Date _3/7/84_

Rating   Comments

5 ▤ 4 ▤ 3 ▤ 2 ▤ 1 ▤
Adaptive ▤   Maladaptive

	Rating	Comments
Personal Causation	4	proud of kids + job, anticipates being successful. assertiveness improving
Values and Goals	4	values job + children, plans to return to work, do more activities
Interests	3	bowls weekly, goes to movies + parties on occassion
Roles	4	claims clerk - counts checks, answer bills, use computer, help out
Habits	3	works, cooks, tv, gets high, somewhat well-organized schedule
Skills	3	does job o.k., learning typing would increase options, skills limit perf.
Output	3	works, no leisure, not satisfied
Physical Environment	3	money problems + limited facilities wants to exercise
Social Environment	3	her children are important (14 + 16) give advice to stop drinking, sometimes she objects
Feedback	3	some self-reflection, main change coming to hospital, doesn't want to be like friends

System Analysis: Global Assessments

	Rating	Comments
Dynamic (Gestalt Functioning)	3	output is minimal, somewhat disatisfied - a few interests but not child related, still has job
Historical (Life History Pattern)	3	feels history was worse at certain times, work maintains best functioning
Contextual (Environmental Influence)	3	occupational behavior somewhat congruent with environment. Needs more social support + community resources
System Trajectory (Occupational Prognosis)	2	currently in a recurring maladaptive cycle, OT needed to reorganize

Comments on Case One: Adrianne

The interview was challenging in terms of Adrianne's slowness to respond, her difficulty answering some questions, and other symptoms of her depression. Making the ratings required some deliberation on certain variables. For instance, some of the raters who rated this interview during the research study rated habits "4" because they said she worked but had few leisure activities. Likewise, some rated personal causation a "4" because of her confidence about skills and her expectation to be successful. Because of these two ratings, they rated dynamic a "4" as they saw her volitional system in line with her output and her goals as realistic. As mentioned earlier, slight discrepancies on a few items would not necessarily make the reliability of the total score unstable. Just as two therapists may clinically view a patient differently and still provide relevant treatment.

The important part in learning to use this instrument is for you to examine the decision making process and try to be as consistent as possible. The question remains, how can this information help in the treatment and discharge planning process?

First, the instrument provides a way to summarize the patient's strengths and weaknesses. For Adrianne, having a few fairly realistic goals, maintaining a job, and identifying several interests are strengths. Her weaknesses include her limited interpersonal skills and difficulty making changes, especially in regard to alcohol. She has the stress of being a single parent with very little adult support noted. She is open to increasing her level of participation in exercise and developing other interests.

Second, this information can be used to assess her level of functioning and select a level of treatment. According to the model of human occupation, occupational behavior spans a continuum of three levels of accomplishment and arousal: exploration, competence, and achievement. (Helpful resources on this topic are chapter 5, "Occupational Function and Dysfunction" in A *Model of Human Occupation*[1] and the second part of the article on the case analysis method by Cubie and Kaplan[2]. These correspond to three maladaptive patterns from helplessness to incompetence and inefficacy (See Figure 7.1).

Adrianne is seen as functioning at the level of incompetence. She is currently having difficulty performing routinely and adequately outside of the hospital. Within the treatment setting she shows some impairment of skills, habits, roles, and volition. However, she is able to collaborate in setting treatment goals and participate in the treatment program. For these reasons she was referred to groups in the inpatient program organized at the competence level. Groups such as task group and leisure awareness group are designed to help patients expand their skills and interests and develop more specific goals and needs.

Initially, due to the extent of her depression, she was involved in treatment groups that increased her activity level, supported her interests, and provided an opportunity for social interaction. Later, she was offered choices when planning her daily schedule to increase her interests and investment in the environment.

During her two and a half week hospitalization, she attended task group and exercise group consistently. At first, she complained of having trouble getting started on activities and relied on the therapist for direction and support. By the time she left, she was more organized and interactive. Her discharge plan included involvement with AA, and exercise group, and a single parent support group. She also continued anti-depressant medication and outpatient psychotherapy.

Eight month follow-up information revealed that although she was still working and living with her children, she had stopped going to AA and her exercise class. She continued to bowl once

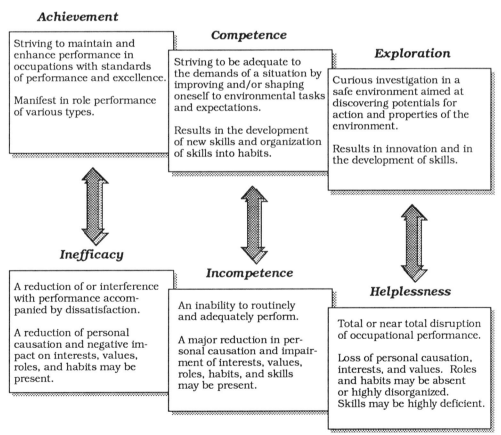

Figure 7.1
Levels of Function and Dysfunction

Adapted from Kielhofner, G. (Ed.), (1985), *A Model of Human Occupation: Theory and Application*, Baltimore: Williams and Wilkins, pp. 65, 70.

a week, but without maintaining her social supports; her depressive and dependent behavior patterns were recurring.

While an instrument such as the OCAIRS can help think through a coherent plan for community adjustment, successful personal change is often an elusive process that requires a more extensive system of psychosocial rehabilitation than is available or feasible. Probably a referral to a day treatment program would have helped Adrianne maintain the gains made in the hospital and offered support for changing her job through follow-up by Vocational Rehabilitation.

Case Two: Jasmine

1. Have your second set of photocopied forms ready.

2. Read the introduction to *Case Two: Jasmine* and the Chart Review and Background Information on page 88.

3. Close the manual and take notes on the interview on the Occupational Case Analysis Interview and Rating Scale Form as you listen to the second case, Jasmine, on side two of the audiotape.

4. When the interview is completed, review the data and make the ratings for each area listed on the same form. Refer to Table 4.1 for additional information regarding rating scale guidelines.

5. Enter your ratings and comments supporting your ratings on the OCAIRS Summary Form. Be alert to recording the ratings in the sequence of the model, not the sequence on the OCAIRS Summary Form.

6. Now return to pages 89–103 in the manual and compare your interview notes, ratings, and summary comments with the handwritten forms. These reflect the assessment of a therapist experienced in using the OCAIRS and allow you an opportunity for self-study.

7. Continue reading about Case Two in the *Comments* section for Jasmine, which includes treatment recommendations and issues related to using the instrument with this example (pages 104–105).

8. Listen to the discussion following the second case on side two of the audiotape.

Introduction to Jasmine

Jasmine walked quickly, though unevenly, to the interview room in a fake leopard coat and heavy make-up. Her speech was pressured and somewhat confrontational. She seemed willing to participate due to the relevance of the interview for her treatment program and her relationship with the interviewer.

Occupational Case Analysis
Interview and Rating Scale
Chart Review and Background Information Form

Chart Review

Patient Name _Jasmine_   Therapist _____
                                      Team _____

Address _____
        _____
        _____

Age _66_   Sex _F_   Race _B_

Date of Admission _March 6, 1984_

Diagnosis _Bipolar Affective Disorder, manic phase_

  Reason for admission, precipitants _on medical unit - taking_
     food + belongings from others
     belligerent when unsupervised

  Previous psychiatric history _first manic episode in 1959,_
  many hospitalizations
  _____

  Condition (mental status, pertinent medical history) _↓ sleep, ↑ energy,_
  pressured speech, euphoria, outlandish
  attire - Diabetes, hypertension, mild renal failure

  Medications _Haldol, clonidine, insulin, lasix_

  Family of origin _5 siblings, many in family "like her"_
                                        hypomanic baseline

Background Information

Living situation: (House)/apartment   (Own)/rent
                   Alone   (With Someone)

  How long _8 yrs_   Plans to move _no_

Highest grade completed _12_

  Classes now (fun, training, self improvement) _Day Care centers -_
  5 days a week, plans to continue

Work _yes, before married - 43 years ago - crossing guard_

  How long _5 yrs_   Plans to change _stopped when married_
                           5 boys, 2 girls - grown

Reason for hospitalization _diabetes, high blood pressure,_
  fluid around ankles
  _____

Interests

- How do you like to spend your time?

  *ride, dance, play cards
  play "numbers"*

- Do you have any other special interests?

  eat, dress

- How often do you participate?

  every day

Rating

⑤ Identifies a variety (four or more) of satisfying interests; two activities pursued regularly.

4 Identifies a variety (four or more) of satisfying interests; participation is variable.

3 Identifies a few (one to three) interests; one activity pursued regularly.

2 Identifies a few (one to three) interests; no particular activity is pursued on a regular basis.

1 Does not identify any interests.

Roles

- When people ask you what you do, what do you tell them?

  go to day care

- What kind of responsibilities do you have as a *day care participant*?

  (Fill in "role" from previous response or from demographic information obtained earlier.)

  be there
  they pick me up
  hot lunch
  do games - participate

Rating

5 Realistically describes many (five or more) activities or obligations of a primary role.

(4) Realistically describes several (three to four) activities or obligations of a primary role.

3 Realistically describes one or two activities or obligations of a primary role.

2 Somewhat realistically (or vaguely) describes the activities or obligations of a primary role.

1 Does not describe a primary role.

Habits

- Do you generally have a daily schedule that lets you do the things you need to do and want to do?

  yes

- Tell me what it is like.

  bowling, sewing, drawing, knitting
  up at 5:00 am, sleep 10:00 pm
  weekends - same, go to church
  play numbers

- Over the past 6 months to a year, has there been a change in how you spend your time?

  no

  (If yes...) What is the change and how do you feel about it?

Rating

5 Describes a very well-organized daily schedule of valued activities. There is a balance among work, leisure, and self-maintenance activities.

4 Describes a pretty well-organized daily schedule of valued activities. However, there are either no leisure or no work activities mentioned.

③ Describes a somewhat well-organized daily schedule of activities (not necessarily valued). The report is somewhat disjointed.

2 Describes a minimally organized daily schedule of activities. The person does not do very much in a day.

1 Does not describe a daily schedule of activities.

Skills

- In your daily activities, what things do you know how to do well?

  cook, wash, iron, clean up

  — How well do you feel you get along with people?

  wonderful, lots of friends

  — How about making decisions and solving problems?

  if cl can't have my way, cl push + fight

  — Do you have any physical limitations or anything that keeps you from doing activities you want to do?

  no

- In order to do the activities you are interested in, are there any skills you feel you need to improve or want to learn?

  no

Rating

5 Has adequate skills for all of current and projected activities. Mostly wants to improve skills to increase already competent and enjoyable activities.

4 Has adequate skills for most of current and projected activities. However, to be satisfied in leisure or work would need to learn some new skill(s).

(3) Has adequate skills for some of current and projected activities. However, level of skills limit optimal performance. Manner of responding is rather global (vague) or too focused (concrete).

2 Has adequate skills for few of current and projected activities. Level of skills impedes ability to work or have a productive role. Response may not totally make sense.

1 Does not identify skills.

Output

- Overall, how satisfied are you with how you spend your time?

  wonderful

- Do you feel your daily routine allows you to use your skills to the best of your ability?

  yes, when husband gets home...

- Are there things you would like to do but you do not get a chance?

  no

Rating

⑤ Integrates all of skills and routines into competent and satisfying occupational behavior. Participates in work and leisure activities.

4 Integrates most of skills and routines into competent and somewhat satisfying behavior. Patient works but does not participate in leisure activities.

3 Integrates some of skills and routines into competent behavior, but may not be satisfied. Either works or is involved in leisure but not both.

2 Integrates few of skills and routines into competent or satisfying occupational behavior. Usually is not satisfied and not using skills.

1 Does not report degree of satisfaction with occupational behavior.

Physical Environment

- Are there any activities you do not participate in because you do not have enough money?

  no

  — Or transportation to get there?

    no problem

  — Or there are not facilities in your home or neighborhood?

    no problem

Rating

(5) Physical environment supports the performance of valued activities very well. No problems mentioned.

4 Physical environment supports the performance of valued activities pretty well. One problem mentioned.

3 Physical environment supports the performance of valued activities to some extent. Two problems mentioned.

2 Physical environment supports the performance of valued activities very poorly. Problems have a major consequence (e.g., cannot make ends meet).

1 Does not describe physical environment or says there are no problems in a resistant/non-cooperative manner.

Social Environment

- Who are the most important people in your life right now?

  husband, children, grandchildren, great-grandchild, sisters

- What do they think you ought to do?

  just what I'm doing

- Do you agree with them?

  yes, except for numbers - they do

Rating

5 Values and attitudes of significant others support successful role performance very much. Comments reflect active support of patient's goals and some collaboration in daily life.

④ Values and attitudes of significant others support successful role performance pretty much. Comments reflect general support of patient and less involvement in daily life.

3 Values and attitudes of significant others support successful role performance somewhat. Attitude is mostly judgmental and advice giving (e.g. mostly "shoulds").

2 Values and attitudes of significant others support successful role performance very little. There is lack of interest in and involvement with the patient.

1 Does not identify values and attitudes.

Feedback

- How do you know when it is time for you to make a change?

  when cI'm not satisfied with what cI'm doing

- Are there things or people that affect your making a change?

  my children + husband they tell me to stay home 1 day a week + clean up

- How do you use information or feedback from others to make changes?

  state my opinion + stick to it

Rating

5 Uses feedback to make adaptive changes very well. Patient seeks support from others and makes adaptive changes.

4 Uses feedback to make adaptive changes pretty well. Patient seeks advice from others and makes some changes, although less consistently adaptive.

3 Uses feedback to make adaptive changes to some extent. Patient demonstrates some self-reflection but only makes a few changes.

② Uses feedback to make adaptive changes minimally. Patient demonstrates little self-reflection and is largely unsuccessful in making changes.

1 Does not describe the use of feedback.

Historical

- Overall, do you feel you have had the usual ups and downs or do you feel your past has been exceptionally better or worse than that?

    ups & downs

- What are some examples of when you were doing the best?

    when children were working - educated selves for college

- How old were you during your worst times? What was going on then?

    25 - 30 yrs old
    husband not working, bills to pay, not home enough
    now - retiring on disability - will be home all day long

Rating

5 Perceives all of past functioning as adaptive. Patient has been doing well for a long time, no real low points aside from the usual ups and downs.

④ Perceives most of past functioning as adaptive. Patient has been doing well for a long time but currently has a problem. May identify one example of a worst time which the individual perceives as traumatic.

3 Perceives some of past functioning as adaptive. Patient is currently having difficulty and cites several examples of problematic times in the past.

2 Perceives little of past functioning as adaptive. Patient has been having difficulty for a long time fairly consistently. Patient does not mention any examples of past good times and has no productive role currently.

1 Does not identify how perceives past functioning.

Personal Causation

- What accomplishments, skills, or talents are you most proud of?

  social security, 2 houses, housewife

- Are there any activities you do in which you lack confidence or feel unsuccessful?

  no

- Have you taken any steps toward developing your skills or confidence in this area?

  no

- Over the next few months, how successful do you think you will be?

  go to center

Rating

5 Expresses much confidence about abilities and anticipates very successful outcomes of action. Identifies at least three skills proud of, states at least one item is improving, and indicates that anticipates success.

4 Expresses pretty much confidence about abilities and anticipates pretty successful outcomes of action. Identifies one or two skills proud of, states at least one step taken to improve, and indicates that anticipates being somewhat successful.

(3) Expresses some confidence about abilities and anticipates somewhat successful outcomes of action. Identifies one or two skills, no areas or steps taken to improve, and indicates that anticipates being mostly unsuccessful OR lists no areas of unsuccessful performance and is overly confident about skills.

2 Expresses little confidence about abilities and anticipates barely successful outcomes of action. Does not identify anything to be proud of and indicates that anticipates being unsuccessful.

1 Does not express feelings about abilities or outcomes.

Values and Goals

- What things are most important for you, or do you value, in your life?

  money, numbers, food, medication

- What are your goals?

  money

- What are your plans for the next few weeks?

  go back to center
  play my numbers

- What do you see yourself doing one year from now?

  same thing

- What do you see yourself doing 5-10 years from now?

  same thing, but husband will
  be retired

- What have you worked on in the hospital that you feel will help you meet these goals?

  medication, menu - meals

I have asked you a lot of questions. Do you have any comments or questions for me?

Rating

5 Identifies a variety (three or more) plans for the next few weeks. The plans are consistent with patient's values and long- term goals.

4 Identifies a few (one or two) plans. The plans are consistent with values and goals.

③ Identifies a few (one or two of each) related values and plans, but may not mention any goals or may not be consistent with goal(s).

2 Identifies no or vague plans, a few unrelated values, and vague goals.

1 Does not identify any goals, may have a vague plan.

Dynamic

Compare responses (not only ratings) to questions dealing with throughput. For example, compare the volitional subsystem with output. The volitional subsystem includes responses to personal causation, values/goals, and interests. The output assumes use of role performance, routine habits, and level of skills to achieve competence and feel satisfaction. Write a description of these aspects of the individual's functioning to determine how they interact with each other.

Personal causation - overly confident about skills, no desire to improve

Values/Goals - values money + medication, plans are consistent with values, no other goals

Interests - lots of interests met during participation in Day Care Center

Output - schedule organized by Day care Center, housekeeping, + numbers

5 Individual's output is competent and consistent with volitional subsystem. The individual performs valued activities well.

4 Individual's output is moderate and consistent with volitional subsystem. The individual has fairly realistic goals for his or her moderate level of skills and ability to deal with obstacles.

(3) Individual's output is inconsistent with volitional subsystem or has minimal output and volition. The individual has unrealistically high or low expectations compared with skills.

2 Individual's output is incompetent and consistent with volitional subsystem. The individual does not identify realistic plans or a desire to change. Performance is very limited.

1 Unable to determine to what extent the throughput elements interact consistently.

Contextual

Compare responses (not only ratings) from dynamic assessment (above) to physical and social environment and use of feedback. Think about how the individual's abilities and actions are supported by his or her community, work or home situation, and significant relationships. Consider what bearing the individual's use of feedback has on his or her ability to adapt to and function effectively in his or her current environment.

Physical Environment - no problems, day care + community meet her needs

Social Environment - lots of family support

Feedback - head strong about opinions
makes changes if wants to
she's doing what she wants in
day treatment + leisure time

5 Individual's output and volitional subsystem are very congruent with factors present in the usual environment.

④ Individual's output and volitional subsystem are pretty congruent with factors present in the usual environment.

3 Individual's output and volitional subsystem are somewhat congruent with factors present in the usual environment.

2 Individual's output and volitional subsystem are minimally congruent with factors present in the usual environment.

1 Unable to determine to what extent these factors are congruent with the present environment.

System Trajectory

Compare the responses from the historical, dynamic, and contextual system analyses to make a prediction about the system trajectory. Based on your clinical experience and assessment of how the many factors interact with each other in this individual's life, identify to what extent the individual is in an adaptive or maladaptive cycle. Link this assessment to need for occupational therapy services.

> although patient identifies history of being pretty adaptive - chart reveals multiple hospitalizations for manic-depressive episodes. Day care center seems to support interests + skills + organizes day. Patient mentioned husband's retirement + she may have concerns about that - he has history of alcoholism + she's not used to his increased presence at home.

5 Currently in an adaptive cycle and is expected to continue without occupational therapy services.

4 At risk to enter a maladaptive cycle and needs occupational therapy to assess maintenance of organized behavior.

3 Currently in a recent maladaptive cycle and needs occupational therapy services to reorganize.

② Currently in a recurring maladaptive cycle and needs occupational therapy services to reorganize and prevent reoccurrence.

1 Currently in a continuing maladaptive cycle and needs occupational therapy services to learn how to organize.

Occupational Case Analysis
Interview and Rating Scale
Summary Form

Patient __Jasmine__   O.T. Rater __KK__   Date __3|7|84__

Rating

Adaptive 5 ▤ 4 ▤ 3 ▤ 2 ▤ 1 ▤ Maladaptive

Comments

	Rating	Comments
Personal Causation	3	Proud of finances + being a housewife no skills to improve, overly confident
Values and Goals	3	values "numbers", food, money, + medication; plans to return to Day Care; only goal is to have money
Interests	5	many interests pursued regularly dance, cards, numbers, eat, dress
Roles	4	realistically describes role as Day Care participant
Habits	3	somewhat disjointed report of activities, schedule largely organized by Day Care.
Skills	3	adequate for current life style concrete items mentioned
Output	5	for her level of skills - reports satisfaction + competence
Physical Environment	5	no problems identified
Social Environment	4	identifies extended family as largely supportive, sometimes objects to her numbers
Feedback	2	changes when not satisfied, mostly does what she wants, minimal changes

System Analysis: Global Assessments

	Rating	Comments
Dynamic (Gestalt Functioning)	3	overly confident about skills, satisfied with role + daily schedule Participates in interests
Historical (Life History Pattern)	4	mostly sees past functioning as adaptive. One traumatic time almost 40 yrs ago.
Contextual (Environmental Influence)	4	Day care center supports role performance, family supportive in general, maybe concerned about effect of retirement on her.
System Trajectory (Occupational Prognosis)	2	is in a recurring maladaptive cycle OT provides structure + skill

Comments on Case Two: Jasmine

This interview was challenging in terms of Jasmine's pressured speech, tendency to be tangential, and other symptoms of mania. There was more variation in the ratings, due primarily to how much the rater agreed with Jasmine's confident self-evaluation. Habits and skills ranged from 2-4 and this made the rating of output dependent on how the rater viewed her range and use of skills. There was less variability in ratings of the environment and volition, with the exception of personal causation.

The problem with an interview such as this one is that it is easy for the therapist to start to form a view of the patient and carry this through in all of the component ratings. What you should try to do is consider each aspect of the human system in isolation, except where the instructions say otherwise, and then during the system analysis, deal with the complexities and contradictions. What you are trying to piece together is the *alignment* among the many elements that affect occupational functioning. Ask yourself how well the individual's aspirations, actual performance, environmental support, and satisfaction with self and others work in harmony.

What was interesting in the discussion with the raters after viewing the videotape was the consensus on her current overall status (system trajectory) and the nature of the treatment plan. She is seen as in a recurring maladaptive cycle due to her bipolar illness. Her strengths include her usual involvement in a productive role for this stage of her life, her support from the environment socially and physically, and her resiliancy in the face of multiple medical and emotional problems. Her main area of difficulty is her performance subsystem.

Jasmine is seen as functioning at the level of helplessness because her skills are highly deficient. Her recent history reveals she is belligerent when she is frustrated interpersonally. She cannot participate in activities, including concentrating on the interview, without considerable structure and support. She is hyperactive and bizarre at times, painting her face with markers and wearing outlandish outfits. For these reasons she was referred to exploratory level groups, such as Directive Group Therapy[3], designed to help her develop basic skills in a non-threatening, structured setting in which the therapists take the major responsibility for organizing the treatment environment. In addition she was given a specific behavioral plan while on the unit to increase structure throughout the day and reinforce her participation in the activities of daily living. She was also helped to focus on an individual craft project graded to her level.

While some of Jasmine's scores are higher than Adrianne's, Jasmine is functioning at a lower level in terms of engagement in the treatment process. However, when Jasmine is not in the acute phase of her illness, her life is more organized and supportive than Adrianne's, making her community adjustment more successful. Even though her level of skills may be less than Adrianne's, she is able to use more of them in her daily routine. Yet, she would be at greater risk if she lost the support of her husband than Adrianne—who is already functioning on her own. The course of Jasmine's illness suggests recurrence of hospitalizations when experiencing manic or depressive episodes. The role of the occupational therapist and the inpatient program is to offer support and structure during such times. Also helpful is working with her husband and family to address issues of the chronic nature of her illness and the situational changes that arise, such as her husband's retirement and the impact that has.

Concluding Remarks

The value of the OCAIRS is in helping occupational therapists organize their thinking about the factors which influence an individual's adaptation in everyday occupation. The instrument provides a way of appreciating and integrating the unique perspective of each person based on his potential and life situation.

As you conduct more and more interviews, you will see how many different patterns emerge. The concept of adaptation is the key. Some patients we refer to in shorthand as "high functioning" end up revealing grave deficiencies in personal causation, leading them to a much more restricted life than their skills would suggest. Other patients know what they want to do and have the skills to do it, but for some reason have difficulty putting it together. In this case, developing and maintaining habits takes precedence.

Some patients seem to have it all in terms of environmental support, their role, and other external indicators of success, yet they are suicidal or anorexic. Other patients will run circles around you when you interview them because they are verbally facile and used to hiding their true self, possibly due to patterns of early family dysfunction and later addictive behavior.

This instrument is not designed to answer every patient problem or question. It provides one way to sort through the complexity of assessment data commonly found in short-term psychiatric settings. If it helps you appreciate a patient's situation, assess the adaptiveness of his occupational functioning, and develop a relevant and effective plan for treatment and community adjustment, then the OCAIRS is successful in meeting the need to which it is designed to respond.

References

1. Kielhofner, G. (Ed.) (1985), *A Model of Human Occupation: Theory and Application,* Baltimore: Williams and Wilkins.

2. Cubie, S. and Kaplan, K. (1982), "A case analysis method for the model of human occupation," *American Journal of Occupational Therapy,* 36:645-656.

3. Kaplan, K. (1988), *Directive Group Therapy: Innovative Mental Health Treatment,* Thorofare, NJ: SLACK.

Appendix

OCAIRS Forms

This appendix contains the various forms you will need to use the Occupational Case Analysis Interview and Rating Scale. It includes the Chart Review and Background Information Form, the Occupational Case Analysis Interview and Rating Scale Form, and the OCAIRS Summary Form.

Also included is an alternate set of forms that you might wish to use in place of the Occupational Case Analysis Interview and Rating Scale Form. These forms, the Occupational Case Analysis Interview Form and the Occupational Case Analysis Rating Scale Form, have the same information as the combined form, but separate the information in two forms that are condensed in length and in a slightly different format. The alternate forms will meet the needs of users who want fewer pages to refer to when doing the interview and who find it helpful to have all the ratings gathered together. The ratings on this form are in the same order as the summary form rather than the interview questions.

The decision of which forms to use is totally up to the therapist. One may be easier while learning to use the instrument, for use in teaching, or for a particular learning style. Try both forms and see what you prefer. In fact, the list of interview questions in chapter 4 (pages 34–35) may be another way to collect data on the interview, as the therapist can write the responses in the column of space provided. The choice is yours.

Finally, blank forms with the style of the manual forms are included for use in a variety of ways relevant to the instrument and assessment process, for example, as worksheets for writing about the system analyses or as space to develop treatment recommendations and plans.

It may be helpful when photocopying the forms to organize them in binders so that they will be accessible for each interview as needed. Doing the mechanics ahead of time will streamline the assessment process.

Purchasers of this manual have permission of the authors and publisher to make copies of these forms for clinical use with patients only. The forms may not be reproduced for other purposes, and no other parts of the manual may be reproduced.

Occupational Case Analysis
Interview and Rating Scale
Chart Review and Background Information Form

Chart Review

Patient Name _____   Therapist _____
                                          Team   _____

Address   _____

             _____

             _____

Age _____   Sex _____   Race _____

Date of Admission _____

Diagnosis   _____

   Reason for admission, precipitants _____

   _____

   _____

   Previous psychiatric history _____

   _____

   _____

   Condition (mental status, pertinent medical history) _____

   _____

   _____

   Medications_____

   Family of origin _____

Background Information

Living situation: House/apartment   Own/rent
                     Alone   With Someone

   How long   _____   Plans to move   _____

Highest grade completed_____

   Classes now (fun, training, self improvement) _____

   _____

Work _____

   How long _____   Plans to change_____

Reason for hospitalization _____

   _____

   _____

Interests

- How do you like to spend your time?

- Do you have any other special interests?

- How often do you participate?

Rating

5 Identifies a variety (four or more) of satisfying interests; two activities pursued regularly.

4 Identifies a variety (four or more) of satisfying interests; participation is variable.

3 Identifies a few (one to three) interests; one activity pursued regularly.

2 Identifies a few (one to three) interests; no particular activity is pursued on a regular basis.

1 Does not identify any interests.

Roles

- When people ask you what you do, what do you tell them?

- What kind of responsibilities do you have as a _____?

    (Fill in "role" from previous response or from demographic information obtained earlier.)

Rating

5 Realistically describes many (five or more) activities or obligations of a primary role.

4 Realistically describes several (three to four) activities or obligations of a primary role.

3 Realistically describes one or two activities or obligations of a primary role.

2 Somewhat realistically (or vaguely) describes the activities or obligations of a primary role.

1 Does not describe a primary role.

Habits

- Do you generally have a daily schedule that lets you do the things you need to do and want to do?

- Tell me what it is like.

- Over the past 6 months to a year, has there been a change in how you spend your time?

    (If yes...) What is the change and how do you feel about it?

Rating

5 Describes a very well-organized daily schedule of valued activities. There is a balance among work, leisure, and self-maintenance activities.

4 Describes a pretty well-organized daily schedule of valued activities. However, there are either no leisure or no work activities mentioned.

3 Describes a somewhat well-organized daily schedule of activities (not necessarily valued). The report is somewhat disjointed.

2 Describes a minimally organized daily schedule of activities. The person does not do very much in a day.

1 Does not describe a daily schedule of activities.

Skills

- In your daily activities, what things do you know how to do well?

    — How well do you feel you get along with people?

    — How about making decisions and solving problems?

    — Do you have any physical limitations or anything that keeps you from doing activities you want to do?

- In order to do the activities you are interested in, are there any skills you feel you need to improve or want to learn?

Rating

5 Has adequate skills for all of current and projected activities. Mostly wants to improve skills to increase already competent and enjoyable activities.

4 Has adequate skills for most of current and projected activities. However, to be satisfied in leisure or work would need to learn some new skill(s).

3 Has adequate skills for some of current and projected activities. However, level of skills limit optimal performance. Manner of responding is rather global (vague) or too focused (concrete).

2 Has adequate skills for few of current and projected activities. Level of skills impedes ability to work or have a productive role. Response may not totally make sense.

1 Does not identify skills.

Output

- Overall, how satisfied are you with how you spend your time?

- Do you feel your daily routine allows you to use your skills to the best of your ability?

- Are there things you would like to do but you do not get a chance?

Rating

5 Integrates all of skills and routines into competent and satisfying occupational behavior. Participates in work and leisure activities.

4 Integrates most of skills and routines into competent and somewhat satisfying behavior. Patient works but does not participate in leisure activities.

3 Integrates some of skills and routines into competent behavior, but may not be satisfied. Either works or is involved in leisure but not both.

2 Integrates few of skills and routines into competent or satisfying occupational behavior. Usually is not satisfied and not using skills.

1 Does not report degree of satisfaction with occupational behavior.

Physical Environment

- Are there any activities you do not participate in because you do not have enough money?

  — Or transportation to get there?

  — Or there are not facilities in your home or neighborhood?

Rating

5 Physical environment supports the performance of valued activities very well. No problems mentioned.

4 Physical environment supports the performance of valued activities pretty well. One problem mentioned.

3 Physical environment supports the performance of valued activities to some extent. Two problems mentioned.

2 Physical environment supports the performance of valued activities very poorly. Problems have a major consequence (e.g., cannot make ends meet).

1 Does not describe physical environment or says there are no problems in a resistant/non-cooperative manner.

Social Environment

- Who are the most important people in your life right now?

- What do they think you ought to do?

- Do you agree with them?

Rating

5 Values and attitudes of significant others support successful role performance very much. Comments reflect active support of patient's goals and some collaboration in daily life.

4 Values and attitudes of significant others support successful role performance pretty much. Comments reflect general support of patient and less involvement in daily life.

3 Values and attitudes of significant others support successful role performance somewhat. Attitude is mostly judgmental and advice giving (e.g. mostly "shoulds").

2 Values and attitudes of significant others support successful role performance very little. There is lack of interest in and involvement with the patient.

1 Does not identify values and attitudes.

Feedback

- How do you know when it is time for you to make a change?

- Are there things or people that affect your making a change?

- How do you use information or feedback from others to make changes?

Rating

5 Uses feedback to make adaptive changes very well. Patient seeks support from others and makes adaptive changes.

4 Uses feedback to make adaptive changes pretty well. Patient seeks advice from others and makes some changes, although less consistently adaptive.

3 Uses feedback to make adaptive changes to some extent. Patient demonstrates some self-reflection but only makes a few changes.

2 Uses feedback to make adaptive changes minimally. Patient demonstrates little self-reflection and is largely unsuccessful in making changes.

1 Does not describe the use of feedback.

Historical

- Overall, do you feel you have had the usual ups and downs or do you feel your past has been exceptionally better or worse than that?

- What are some examples of when you were doing the best?

- How old were you during your worst times? What was going on then?

Rating

5 Perceives all of past functioning as adaptive. Patient has been doing well for a long time, no real low points aside from the usual ups and downs.

4 Perceives most of past functioning as adaptive. Patient has been doing well for a long time but currently has a problem. May identify one example of a worst time which the individual perceives as traumatic.

3 Perceives some of past functioning as adaptive. Patient is currently having difficulty and cites several examples of problematic times in the past.

2 Perceives little of past functioning as adaptive. Patient has been having difficulty for a long time fairly consistently. Patient does not mention any examples of past good times and has no productive role currently.

1 Does not identify how perceives past functioning.

Personal Causation

- What accomplishments, skills, or talents are you most proud of?

- Are there any activities you do in which you lack confidence or feel unsuccessful?

- Have you taken any steps toward developing your skills or confidence in this area?

- Over the next few months, how successful do you think you will be?

Rating

5 Expresses much confidence about abilities and anticipates very successful outcomes of action. Identifies at least three skills proud of, states at least one item is improving, and indicates that anticipates success.

4 Expresses pretty much confidence about abilities and anticipates pretty successful outcomes of action. Identifies one or two skills proud of, states at least one step taken to improve, and indicates that anticipates being somewhat successful.

3 Expresses some confidence about abilities and anticipates somewhat successful outcomes of action. Identifies one or two skills, no areas or steps taken to improve, and indicates that anticipates being mostly unsuccessful OR lists no areas of unsuccessful performance and is overly confident about skills.

2 Expresses little confidence about abilities and anticipates barely successful outcomes of action. Does not identify anything to be proud of and indicates that anticipates being unsuccessful.

1 Does not express feelings about abilities or outcomes.

Values and Goals

- What things are most important for you, or do you value in your life?

- What are your goals?

- What are your plans for the next few weeks?

- What do you see yourself doing one year from now?

- What do you see yourself doing 5 to 10 years from now?

- What have you worked on in the hospital that you feel will help you meet these goals?

I have asked you a lot of questions. Do you have any comments or questions for me?

Rating

5 Identifies a variety (three or more) plans for the next few weeks. The plans are consistent with patient's values and long-term goals.

4 Identifies a few (one or two) plans. The plans are consistent with values and goals.

3 Identifies a few (one or two of each) related values and plans, but may not mention any goals or may not be consistent with goal(s).

2 Identifies no or vague plans, a few unrelated values, and vague goals.

1 Does not identify any goals, may have a vague plan.

Dynamic

Compare responses (not only ratings) to questions dealing with throughput. For example, compare the volitional subsystem with output. The volitional subsystem includes responses to personal causation, values/goals, and interests. The output assumes use of role performance, routine habits, and level of skills to achieve competence and feel satisfaction. Write a description of these aspects of the individual's functioning to determine how they interact with each other.

5 Individual's output is competent and consistent with volitional subsystem. The individual performs valued activities well.

4 Individual's output is moderate and consistent with volitional subsystem. The individual has fairly realistic goals for his moderate level of skills and ability to deal with obstacles.

3 Individual's output is inconsistent with volitional subsystem or has minimal output and volition. The individual has unrealistically high or low expectations compared with skills.

2 Individual's output is incompetent and consistent with volitional subsystem. The individual does not identify realistic plans or a desire to change. Performance is very limited.

1 Unable to determine to what extent the throughput elements interact consistently.

Contextual

Compare responses (not only ratings) from dynamic assessment (above) to physical and social environment and use of feedback. Think about how the individual's abilities and actions are supported by his community, work or home situation, and significant relationships. Consider what bearing the individual's use of feedback has on his ability to adapt to and function effectively in his current environment.

5 Individual's output and volitional subsystem are very congruent with factors present in the usual environment.

4 Individual's output and volitional subsystem are pretty congruent with factors present in the usual environment.

3 Individual's output and volitional subsystem are somewhat congruent with factors present in the usual environment.

2 Individual's output and volitional subsystem are minimally congruent with factors present in the usual environment.

1 Unable to determine to what extent these factors are congruent with the present environment.

System Trajectory

Compare the responses from the historical, dynamic, and contextual system analyses to make a prediction about the system trajectory. Based on your clinical experience and assessment of how the many factors interact with each other in this individual's life, identify to what extent the individual is in an adaptive or maladaptive cycle. Link this assessment to need for occupational therapy services.

5 Currently in an adaptive cycle and is expected to continue without occupational therapy services.

4 At risk to enter a maladaptive cycle and needs occupational therapy to assess maintenance of organized behavior.

3 Currently in a recent maladaptive cycle and needs occupational therapy services to reorganize.

2 Currently in a recurring maladaptive cycle and needs occupational therapy services to reorganize and prevent reoccurrence.

1 Currently in a continuing maladaptive cycle and needs occupational therapy services to learn how to organize.

Occupational Case Analysis
Interview and Rating Scale
Summary Form

Patient _____ O.T. Rater _____ Date _____

Rating   **Comments**

5☰ **4**☰ **3**☰ **2**☰ **1**☰

Adaptive   Maladaptive

Personal Causation		
Values and Goals		
Interests		
Roles		
Habits		
Skills		
Output		
Physical Environment		
Social Environment		
Feedback		

System Analysis: Global Assessments

Dynamic (Gestalt Functioning)		
Historical (Life History Pattern)		
Contextual (Environmental Influence)		
System Trajectory (Occupational Prognosis)		

Interests

- How do you like to spend your time?

- Do you have any other special interests?

- How often do you participate?

Roles

- When people ask you what you do, what do you tell them?

- What kind of responsibilities do you have as a _____?

  (Fill in "role" from previous response or from demographic information obtained earlier.)

Habits

- Do you generally have a daily schedule that lets you do the things you need to do and want to do?

- Tell me what it is like.

- Over the past 6 months to a year, has there been a change in how you spend your time?

  (If yes...) What is the change and how do you feel about it?

Skills

- In your daily activities, what things do you know how to do well?

  — How well do you feel you get along with people?

  — How about making decisions and solving problems?

  — Do you have any physical limitations or anything that keeps you from doing activities you want to do?

- In order to do the activities you are interested in, are there any skills you feel you need to improve or want to learn?

Output

- Overall, how satisfied are you with how you spend your time?

- Do you feel your daily routine allows you to use your skills to the best of your ability?

- Are there things you would like to do but you do not get a chance?

Physical Environment

- Are there any activities you do not participate in because you do not have enough money?

  — Or transportation to get there?

  — Or there are not facilities in your home or neighborhood?

Social Environment

- Who are the most important people in your life right now?

- What do they think you ought to do?

- Do you agree with them?

Feedback

- How do you know when it is time for you to make a change?

- Are there things or people that affect your making a change?

- How do you use information or feedback from others to make changes?

Historical

- Overall, do you feel you have had the usual ups and downs or do you feel your past has been exceptionally better or worse than that?

- What are some examples of when you were doing the best?

- How old were you during your worst times? What was going on then?

Personal Causation

- What accomplishments, skills, or talents are you most proud of?

- Are there any activities you do in which you lack confidence or feel unsuccessful?

- Have you taken any steps toward developing your skills or confidence in this area?

- Over the next few months, how successful do you think you will be?

Values and Goals

- What things are most important for you, or do you value in your life?

- What are your goals?

- What are your plans for the next few weeks?

- What do you see yourself doing one year from now?

- What do you see yourself doing 5 to 10 years from now?

- What have you worked on in the hospital that you feel will help you meet these goals?

I have asked you a lot of questions. Do you have any comments or questions for me?

Personal Causation

5 Expresses much confidence about abilities and anticipates very successful outcomes of action. Identifies at least three skills proud of, states at least one item is improving, and indicates that anticipates success.

4 Expresses pretty much confidence about abilities and anticipates pretty successful outcomes of action. Identifies one or two skills proud of, states at least one step taken to improve, and indicates that anticipates being somewhat successful.

3 Expresses some confidence about abilities and anticipates somewhat successful outcomes of action. Identifies one or two skills, no areas or steps taken to improve, and indicates that anticipates being mostly unsuccessful OR lists no areas of unsuccessful performance and is overly confident about skills.

2 Expresses little confidence about abilities and anticipates barely successful outcomes of action. Does not identify anything to be proud of and indicates that anticipates being unsuccessful.

1 Does not express feelings about abilities or outcomes.

Values and Goals

5 Identifies a variety (three or more) plans for the next few weeks. The plans are consistent with patient's values and long-term goals.

4 Identifies a few (one or two) plans. The plans are consistent with values and goals.

3 Identifies a few (one or two of each) related values and plans, but may not mention any goals or may not be consistent with goal(s).

2 Identifies no or vague plans, a few unrelated values, and vague goals.

1 Does not identify any goals, may have a vague plan.

Interests

5 Identifies a variety (four or more) of satisfying interests; two activities pursued regularly.

4 Identifies a variety (four or more) of satisfying interests; participation is variable.

3 Identifies a few (one to three) interests; one activity pursued regularly.

2 Identifies a few (one to three) interests; no particular activity is pursued on a regular basis.

1 Does not identify any interests.

Roles

5 Realistically describes many (five or more) activities or obligations of a primary role.

4 Realistically describes several (three to four) activities or obligations of a primary role.

3 Realistically describes one or two activities or obligations of a primary role.

2 Somewhat realistically (or vaguely) describes the activities or obligations of a primary role.

1 Does not describe a primary role.

Habits

5 Describes a very well-organized daily schedule of valued activities. There is a balance among work, leisure, and self-maintenance activities.

4 Describes a pretty well-organized daily schedule of valued activities. However, there are either no leisure or no work activities mentioned.

3 Describes a somewhat well-organized daily schedule of activities (not necessarily valued). The report is somewhat disjointed.

2 Describes a minimally organized daily schedule of activities. The person does not do very much in a day.

1 Does not describe a daily schedule of activities.

Skills

5 Has adequate skills for all of current and projected activities. Mostly wants to improve skills to increase already competent and enjoyable activities.

4 Has adequate skills for most of current and projected activities. However, to be satisfied in leisure or work would need to learn some new skill(s).

3 Has adequate skills for some of current and projected activities. However, level of skills limit optimal performance. Manner of responding is rather global (vague) or too focused (concrete).

2 Has adequate skills for few of current and projected activities. Level of skills impedes ability to work or have a productive role. Response may not totally make sense.

1 Does not identify skills.

Output

5 Integrates all of skills and routines into competent and satisfying occupational behavior. Participates in work and leisure activities.

4 Integrates most of skills and routines into competent and somewhat satisfying behavior. Patient works but does not participate in leisure activities.

3 Integrates some of skills and routines into competent behavior, but may not be satisfied. Either works or is involved in leisure but not both.

2 Integrates few of skills and routines into competent or satisfying occupational behavior. Usually is not satisfied and not using skills.

1 Does not report degree of satisfaction with occupational behavior.

Physical Environment

5 Physical environment supports the performance of valued activities very well. No problems mentioned.

4 Physical environment supports the performance of valued activities pretty well. One problem mentioned.

3 Physical environment supports the performance of valued activities to some extent. Two problems mentioned.

2 Physical environment supports the performance of valued activities very poorly. Problems have a major consequence (e.g., cannot make ends meet).

1 Does not describe physical environment or says there are no problems in a resistant/non-cooperative manner.

Social Environment

5   Values and attitudes of significant others support successful role performance very much. Comments reflect active support of patient's goals and some collaboration in daily life.

4   Values and attitudes of significant others support successful role performance pretty much. Comments reflect general support of patient and less involvement in daily life.

3   Values and attitudes of significant others support successful role performance somewhat. Attitude is mostly judgmental and advice giving (e.g. mostly "shoulds").

2   Values and attitudes of significant others support successful role performance very little. There is lack of interest in and involvement with the patient.

1   Does not identify values and attitudes.

Feedback

5   Uses feedback to make adaptive changes very well. Patient seeks support from others and makes adaptive changes.

4   Uses feedback to make adaptive changes pretty well. Patient seeks advice from others and makes some changes, although less consistently adaptive.

3   Uses feedback to make adaptive changes to some extent. Patient demonstrates some self-reflection but only makes a few changes.

2   Uses feedback to make adaptive changes minimally. Patient demonstrates little self-reflection and is largely unsuccessful in making changes.

1   Does not describe the use of feedback.

Dynamic

5   Individual's output is competent and consistent with volitional subsystem. The individual performs valued activities well.

4   Individual's output is moderate and consistent with volitional subsystem. The individual has fairly realistic goals for his moderate level of skills and ability to deal with obstacles.

3   Individual's output is inconsistent with volitional subsystem or has minimal output and volition. The individual has unrealistically high or low expectations compared with skills.

2   Individual's output is incompetent and consistent with volitional subsystem. The individual does not identify realistic plans or a desire to change. Performance is very limited.

1   Unable to determine to what extent the throughput elements interact consistently.

Historical

5   Perceives all of past functioning as adaptive. Patient has been doing well for a long time, no real low points aside from the usual ups and downs.

4   Perceives most of past functioning as adaptive. Patient has been doing well for a long time but currently has a problem. May identify one example of a worst time which the individual perceives as traumatic.

3   Perceives some of past functioning as adaptive. Patient is currently having difficulty and cites several examples of problematic times in the past.

2   Perceives little of past functioning as adaptive. Patient has been having difficulty for a long time fairly consistently. Patient does not mention any examples of past good times and has no productive role currently.

1   Does not identify how perceives past functioning.

Contextual

5   Individual's output and volitional subsystem are very congruent with factors present in the usual environment.

4   Individual's output and volitional subsystem are pretty congruent with factors present in the usual environment.

3   Individual's output and volitional subsystem are somewhat congruent with factors present in the usual environment.

2   Individual's output and volitional subsystem are minimally congruent with factors present in the usual environment.

1   Unable to determine to what extent these factors are congruent with the present environment.

System Trajectory

5   Currently in an adaptive cycle and is expected to continue without occupational therapy services.

4   At risk to enter a maladaptive cycle and needs occupational therapy to assess maintenance of organized behavior.

3   Currently in a recent maladaptive cycle and needs occupational therapy services to reorganize.

2   Currently in a recurring maladaptive cycle and needs occupational therapy services to reorganize and prevent reoccurrence.

1   Currently in a continuing maladaptive cycle and needs occupational therapy services to learn how to organize.